THE CONCUSSION *Companion*

THE REAL WORLD GUIDE TO NAVIGATING RECOVERY WITH CONFIDENCE AND CLARITY

Stacey Smith

Get Your Free Bonus

The Companion Workbook:
10 Steps to an Empowered Recovery

To get the best experience with this book, I've found readers who download and use **The Companion Workbook** are able to implement the lessons in this book faster and more easily. Using this workbook will guide you in taking the next steps to creating your path to recovery with confidence and clarity.

Get your copy by visiting:
www.theconcussioncompanion.com/freebonus

For my friends and family
who stuck by me through the wildest ride.

TABLE OF CONTENTS

INTRODUCTION   9

MY STORY   17

PART ONE: GETTING CLEAR

Chapter 1   Understanding Concussions   39

Chapter 2   Recovery 101   55

Chapter 3   Navigating the Medical World   73

PART TWO: ESSENTIALS FOR HEALING

Chapter 4   Hydration, Sleep, and Movement 91

Chapter 5   Nutrition   109

Chapter 6   Managing Your Mindset   125

PART THREE: GETTING THROUGH THE DAYS

Chapter 7   Getting Through the Days   151

Chapter 8   Techniques to Try When You're
                Feeling Stuck   163

Chapter 9   Support   173

Chapter 10 Post-Its   185

Chapter 11 Supplies   193

Chapter 12 Final Thoughts   199

THANKS FOR READING   203

RESOURCES   205

ACKNOWLEDGMENTS   207

NOTES   209

Introduction

The pain was so intense and unrelenting for so long that I didn't know how much longer I could keep hanging on. Sometimes I thought it would be nice to just quietly fade away. I found myself saying to friends and family, "I'm not suicidal, but I don't know how much longer I can do this." The fact that I was beginning to be interested in no longer being alive was terrifying.

Although concussions are classified as "mild" traumatic brain injuries, there is nothing mild about them. They are classified as mild because they are not life-threatening. They can, however, be seriously life-altering. In my case, it ended up being life-altering for the better, but not without a serious and protracted struggle.

At the time of my concussion, I was a political fundraiser. I was stressed, anxious, and a workaholic but also happy and thriving, living the urban millennial dream: condo, cat, boyfriend, book club, international vacations, brunch on the weekends, the works. Over the course of my recovery, this entire life would get dismantled (except for the cat). It was gradual at first, with time for me to acclimate to each step along the way. But eventually, I hit a point where I wasn't willing to let go of the things that were left, namely my job, and the universe stepped in with a sledgehammer to get this roadblock to recovery out of my way. More on this later.

Throughout my recovery, I had the support of an unshakeable network of family, friends, clients, coworkers, neighbors, and an incredibly generous and supportive boss who never let me doubt that they would see me through to the other side. Their unwavering support allowed me to sink to absolute rock bottom without having any doubt that they would hold me up and pull me back when I couldn't do it myself. Eventually, I *did* hit rock bottom, and I learned some interesting things along the way that inspired me to share my story.

Flash forward to four years post-injury and the publication of this book, and I have found my way to health, happiness, passion, purpose, peace, and joy at a level far beyond my pre-injury self. I am still dealing with chronic pain and physical limitations, but somehow these things are able to co-exist. In order to heal from the injury, I had to do deep inner work. Unhealthy habits had to be overhauled, and emotional healing had to be addressed. I had to tap into new levels of faith and purpose to pull me through. All of this took a lot of effort and seeking. In this book, I share with you the information and tools that worked for me in hopes they may support your recovery, too.

While most people recover within a few weeks of their injury, this book is for the more than thirty percent of people who don't. Because without proper guidance and support, long-term recovery can be devastating—physically, emotionally, relationally, and financially. I had a number of questions on a loop in my head throughout the first few years of my recovery.

Is it this hard for everybody else, too?

Am I missing something?

How do people do this? How do they <u>survive</u> it?

This book is my answer to those questions and validation for anyone questioning their experience. It is what I would want to share with you if we were to sit down for coffee at the outset of *your* injury. You'll find it provides a high-level overview of the recovery process and points you in the direction of the best resources I found for different situations and needs. It was my experience that finding my way to these resources was convoluted and difficult, and I rarely found what I needed when I actually needed it. For that reason, I intend to share this book as a road map and information hub.

In the first section, I'll go over the process of recovery as a whole and help you get clear on how it works and what it takes. In the second, I'll cover the essential components your body needs in order to heal, and in the third, I'll provide actionable tools and strategies for making it through the days. Not every tool will help in every situation, and different things work for different people. What you need in one phase of recovery may not be what you need in another. But my hope is what you find here will be a helpful hub to pull from – grabbing onto what's useful and leaving the rest behind – as you build your own recovery plan and toolbox.

This is not a book containing medical advice or specific directives; I am not a medical professional. It is my story of how I made it through and the information and tools I learned along the way through my own seeking and research. This is, in essence, the master file I wish somebody could have handed me in the early days after my injury to help inform and guide my path.

Turning the Corner

It was a year into my recovery, and I was nearing the end of my rope. Panic attacks, cognitive and memory dysfunctions, severe headaches, debilitating overwhelm, a skyrocketing heart rate, dizziness, visual problems, uncontrollable tears, and depression were my daily companions. At the same time, I was trying to hang on to a part time job and pushing myself way past my limit on a daily basis.

I was biding my time between medical appointments, always hoping that at the next one, the doctor would have the medication or treatment that would finally make me "better." My goal was just to hang on a little longer until I got the break I needed.

I remember very clearly the day I turned a corner.

One day, while meditating, which I relied on for pain and anxiety management, I had the experience of feeling myself lying face down, flat on my stomach, on what I can only describe as feeling like the floor of the universe. It was dark. It was still. It was quiet. It wasn't scary; it felt safe and calm there. But it was very far down. I can still feel myself pressing against the bottom when I think of it now. It was the strangest experience, and I have no idea how I got there. I don't even know where I was exactly. All I know is that I felt completely certain that I could not go down any further. I was at the actual bottom.

I could sense that on the other side of whatever I was pressed down against was "the other side," and I knew I wasn't meant to go there. I also knew I didn't have any energy left to get myself back up. So, I let go, not by choice, but because I simply didn't have anything left to hold on with. I could feel the moment of release when I was all used up, and that's when I started feeling myself slowly float back up.

It was so gentle and natural. I was only able to start floating because I had finally stopped hanging on so tight. Finally, nature could step in and take over, and it's like she had been waiting in the wings the whole time, patiently awaiting her turn at the wheel. I started working in sync with my body's natural desire and ability to heal itself and finally stopped working against the process. It's worth noting that I didn't know I *had* been working against it until things started flowing differently. In that moment I realized that I had been pushing myself so hard I had actually been blocking healing.

I could feel a realignment in my body, like something had clicked into place, and healing energy could finally flow. I still go back to this feeling of alignment as a visualization tool when I'm anxious or in pain, and it's powerful. I will share more about it later in the book.

From then on, I understood that in addition to the medical aspects of my recovery program, my job was to create space for my body to heal. I needed to slow down. Give myself time and permission to rest both physically and mentally, without pushing so hard, and generally get out of the way and let my body do its thing.

It didn't exactly get easier after that, but I felt like I was finally on the right track. It's almost as if my recovery didn't start until this happened.

Finding Purpose

I kept myself motivated over the years that followed with the thought that on the other side of recovery, whatever that looked like, I would put together everything I learned along the way, from how to find the proper medical care, to how to manage the day-to-day challenges and make it available to anyone else experiencing the confusion or desperation that I was experiencing. It is unfathomable to me that each year, millions of people experience a concussion, yet it's such an unknown, isolating, and bewildering experience for so many. I kept notes on the questions I couldn't find answers to, intending to revisit them when I could do the research. I filled multiple notebooks and countless voice memos with notes and questions to address here, hoping it might make a difference for you.

I share all of this to explain why I wrote this book. I don't know that I can make your recovery any less painful, and I certainly don't have all the answers, but I do hope to help you feel less lost and alone. If there's a chance that this book might help even one person struggle just a little less, writing it will have been worth it.

My hope is that you have a quick and straightforward recovery and that your concussion is only a small blip on the radar—no floor of the universe for you. But if, like me, you draw a long recovery, I hope what you find in these pages will help you feel empowered to navigate a messy situation with the confidence that you aren't making it up and that, yes, it really is this difficult for other people too.

Some of this content may be relevant to you now, and some not until later. I hope this is a book you will come back to over time as you work your way through different stages. If there is one thing I want to share right up front, it's that *you cannot force recovery*. But you can guide the process with faith and resilience, and you can learn to be good to yourself along the way. This makes all the difference.

Let's dive in.

My Story

"When life is sweet, say 'thank you' and celebrate,
and when life is bitter, say 'thank you' and grow."
—Shauna Niequist

In July 2019, I was water-skiing while on vacation with my family in Minnesota. One of my skis caught in the wake while I was cutting in and out, and I fell forward at a high speed. The left side of my forehead hit the water and took the impact. When I came up for air, I saw stars and felt disoriented. I also immediately checked that my earrings were still in (they were) and that my lifejacket was still secure (it wasn't). The force of the impact had caused it to come almost completely unzipped.

After reorienting myself and putting my skis back on, I shouted, "Hit it!" and finished out my run. I was breathless, dazed, and had a *severe* headache. As we neared the dock, we hit a choppy patch of water, and bumping over each wave caused pounding pain in my head. Afterward, I was nauseous, unsteady, and felt a little detached from everything around me. But I was on vacation, surrounded by my family, who I love and adore being with, and I figured the best thing to do was paste on a smile and ignore the pain. I was aware that I felt extremely out of it but figured I just needed a little time to recover from the shock of the fall.

Over the course of the day, things got weird. I was hit with overwhelming sadness, seemingly out of nowhere. Not typical for vacation. When I was around people, it felt like I was surrounded by a bubble of fog that kept me from truly engaging. Pain engulfed me. Interacting with people made me dizzy, and I felt almost like I was having an out-of-body experience.

I was also easily irritated, which is unusual for me. I am a people person. But now, when people talked to me, I was in so much pain and so nauseous that I had to excuse myself from the conversation (sometimes without any explanation at all because I was too disoriented to find something to say). I was also anxious, depressed, and confused about how I was feeling. I felt isolated and alone, even though I was surrounded by my people. This continued for a few days, and I didn't connect it to the fall. In my bedroom that night and the next, I cried from the pain and worried about how I would drive myself the 10-plus hours back to Chicago if something didn't change. I was not much of a crier before the accident.

The thought of a concussion never entered my mind. They don't teach you about concussions in my line of work. Over the remainder of the vacation, I took some Advil but, otherwise, carried on as best I could.

If I'd had my normal cognition and executive functioning, I would've been able to recognize and communicate that something was seriously wrong. But those skills were not available to me and would remain unreachable for a very long time.

The First Few Weeks

Two days later, I was still in severe pain and deeply nervous about my drive home. I was still feeling detached and dazed, but it never occurred to me to share this with anyone. I knew I was feeling off, but I couldn't put my finger on exactly what was happening, so I got in the car. The trip took close to 11 hours, and by some miracle, I made it safely.

At this time, I was mentoring a young girl, and I was committed to taking her swimming over the coming weekend. I was nauseous and in pain, but we loved to swim together, and a headache is no reason to cancel plans, right? I miscalculated. Being at a pool with sunlight reflecting off the water, sounds from the kids reverberating off the walls, the frenetic motion of the waves, and kids jumping and splashing were nearly unbearable. I spent most of the time standing by myself with my eyes closed, doing deep breathing, and trying not to throw up. But again, I pushed through.

The following Monday morning, I attempted to work from home. My head was pounding. My thoughts weren't processing like normal. I couldn't focus. I figured I was just slowly getting back into the swing of things after vacation.

Then three days after I got home, five days after the accident, a friend who is a teacher and was trained in these things suggested I might have a concussion. I replied with something along the lines of "What? I don't even really know what that is."

After a quick google search, the lightbulb turned on, and I sought help immediately. Actually, what I did first was call my mom, who is a nurse. *Is this a big deal? Do I need to get it checked out?* Yes, and yes. My mom had been with me on the trip and saw the fall but had not considered that I may have sustained a concussion. I mentioned a few times that I had a headache, but I never let my family know the severity of the pain and dysfunction I was experiencing.

When I got to urgent care, they went through the CDC's concussion symptom checklist with me, and I started crying. I was responding "yes" to every single item and understanding that I'd been experiencing symptoms I had no idea were due to an injury: irritability, depression, anxiety, sensitivity to motion and sound, nausea, dizziness, impaired sleep, difficulty focusing my eyes on just about anything, difficulty concentrating, and more.

Because of the severity with which I responded to the symptom assessment, I was advised to go directly to the emergency room to make sure I didn't have a brain bleed. They offered to call an ambulance for me, but I declined because that seemed dramatic. I asked if I could drive myself, and they looked at me like I was crazy. I still didn't understand the scope of what was happening. I took a cab.

At the emergency room, my CT scan was clear. They sent me home with a few ice packs, heat packs, and instructions to take Tylenol for pain, get lots of rest, and follow up with my primary care doctor in a week.

I went home having no idea I was experiencing a serious injury and completely unprepared for the long-haul recovery that was to follow. I still thought it was just a bump on the head and didn't understand that my brain was truly *injured*. The instructions from my primary care doctor the following week were to rest until things started calming down, but ... they didn't.

The First Few Months

For the next few months, I stayed at home, completely incapacitated. I spent many, many days in bed and, on a good day, would move to the couch for a few hours, most of the time with my eye mask on. Some days, I could not handle any light or sound at all. I was not working during this time. I was waiting for my symptoms and pain to start subsiding. It was nowhere in my field of awareness that this could (and would) go on for years. Family and friends stayed with me for support, to keep food in front of me, and to go out with me for very slow walks when I was able. The best I can describe this time is bewildering. I was dizzy all the time and felt disconnected from my ability to think clearly.

My boyfriend and I broke up shortly after my trip to the emergency room, and I was intensely angry and sad. The injury heightened these emotions to very high levels.

One afternoon, a car alarm went off outside my apartment, making my pain so unbearable that I started swearing out the window in anger. Loud noises were more than loud noises. I could feel them reverberating throughout my head and body, and I no longer had the emotional control that I used to.

I kept checking in with my doctor every two weeks, and after a while was referred to a neurologist and a specialized psychiatrist for neuropsychological testing. My doctor explained that my pre-injury history of migraines, depression, and anxiety could be triggered and worsened by the injury and may take a long time to heal, but the reality of what that meant still didn't sink in.

The neurologist prescribed a migraine medication for the headaches, and both she and the psychiatrist thought I did not need the neuro-psych testing. Since it would have been expensive, and wasn't deemed necessary by the specialists, I passed. At the time, I didn't understand that the testing would have helped identify my cognitive deficits, demonstrated clearly that there were issues, pointed me to cognitive rehabilitation therapies, and helped guide a return-to-work plan. This was not explained to me. I still expected that my symptoms would resolve soon on their own, so I continued to ride it out.

Going Back to Work

After three months, it felt like it was time to get back to work part-time. I had improved some, and with so much time having passed, I felt like full recovery was surely just around the corner. I can see now that I was nowhere near ready to work, but those three months felt like forever at the time. Before the accident, I was hard-charging, motivated, and highly successful in my career. The thought of slowing down or not working after already having taken three months off did not compute for me. I figured I would just suck it up and keep going until things got better.

Starting back to work did not go well, to say the least. Even the most basic tasks were incredibly taxing on my brain. It took me roughly triple the time to complete simple things; my memory was impaired, and I couldn't follow tasks that required more than one step or any strategic thinking. I could not hold a thought in my head, and I would be completely exhausted after even an hour of work. When people asked me how I was doing, I often involuntarily started crying. It was not a good look, and I couldn't do anything to stop it.

At the time, I was senior vice president of a political fundraising consulting firm. My work involved managing multiple clients, mentoring staff, and keeping up in a fast-paced, aggressive environment. On a day-to-day basis, I communicated with and managed campaign support from elected officials, CEOs, philanthropists, and civic leaders. I managed spreadsheets, strategy, and outreach to hundreds of people daily and stayed up to speed with multiple candidates and their campaign needs. In addition, I frequently coordinated and attended cocktail receptions and events for more than a hundred people at a time, smiling and interacting with every person in the room. This was taxing work before my injury, yet I attempted to push through with my impairments, always thinking I needed to hang on just a little bit longer until things got better.

Pushing Through

Even though I was working, I was by no means functioning normally, and it was not business as usual. I had the benefit of being able to work from home some of the time, which gave me a leg up on avoiding overly stimulating environments (anywhere with lights, noise, or other people). On days when I traveled to the office, I would be nauseous and in severe pain by the time I arrived. Riding the train was brutal, but driving wasn't safe due to my vestibular impairment. My eyes weren't tracking properly, and they didn't keep up when I turned my head from side to side. Yet through all of this, most of the time, you couldn't tell anything was wrong from the outside. I was able to put on a smile when it mattered. But I felt like a ghost, or like I was having an out-of-body experience, just trying to go through the motions to get through each day. It's amazing how far our bodies will reach for energy to put on a performance if we demand them to. But this comes at a high cost and, most definitely, at the expense of progress.

After pushing through four months of managing less than half of my usual workload, I had to scale back my responsibilities further because my cognition was still slow, my brain was still foggy, and the headaches were debilitating with visual and cognitive stimulation (the threshold for this was very low). However, I was slowly improving with physical therapy focused on balance and vestibular issues, eye exercises, cognitive activities, and manual work on my neck. We were making progress, and I had been told it could take a long time, so this all seemed normal. It seemed like the best thing to do was stay the course and continue riding it out until I was better. I forced myself through this for more than a year, always hoping that "better" was just around the corner.

Hitting Rock Bottom

I was struggling so significantly a year into my recovery that I moved in with my mom in Iowa for support and to try to keep up appearances at work. I was only handling a very small part-time role at that point, scaled back substantially from my previous position. I was working from home no more than two hours per day, and still, it was impossible to maintain. Keeping up the illusion came at an incredibly steep price that nobody at work could see.

Almost every day after completing my work in the morning, struggling through severe pain and cognitive impairments, I would spend the remainder of the afternoon and evening in bed, with my eye mask on, almost always in tears from pain and anxiety. I was not able to handle making my own meals or any other aspects of managing life. I was surviving, but barely.

At that time, I was running around to three or four appointments per week of physical therapy, dry needling, and acupuncture. I was taking multiple medications for pain and migraine management, trying to do everything I could to move my recovery forward in addition to, and around my work obligations. This was after a full year of treatments already. What I was actually doing was running myself ragged, burning out, and dosing my body with uncomfortably high amounts of medications for pain relief.

This is when I had my "floor of the universe" moment, what I considered my rock bottom, and the situation became untenable. I understood that I needed to let go of some things in order to create more space for healing. This meant fewer appointments, less work, less stress, less pain medication, less biting on a stick and pushing through. I knew that I would need to scale back work even further and that if I eventually had to quit working entirely, I would do whatever it took to get my recovery on track. But I still wasn't ready to go all in. I scaled back my workload again, but I was so emotionally attached to my work, not to mention my financial needs and fears, that I could not let go completely. I decided to sell my car, thinking that having a few extra months of cash for living expenses in the bank would alleviate my stress and give me a long enough runway in case I did need to step away from work for a while.

In hindsight, should I have been working? No. But I *wanted* to be working. My entire identity and purpose revolved around the career I had built. There were also financial implications. I had enough saved to last me a while, but

I was worried about the long-term and the high cost of my medical care. I also didn't fully understand that work was standing in the way of my recovery, even though two of my providers told me this could be the case. I had no idea that some people actually have to quit their jobs; I thought people just toughed it out.

Throughout this time, I went to the standard medical providers and worked through the usual treatment protocols for my symptoms, mainly physical therapy and medication for pain. I worked with multiple doctors, neurologists, physical therapists, a talk therapist, and an acupuncturist to explore pain management options, but nothing brought it under control. We tried increasing doses of nortriptyline, multiple fast-acting migraine medications, every combination of over-the-counter pain relievers, medical marijuana, old-school antidepressants, and blood pressure medications known to help migraines, monthly migraine injections, trigger point injections, a muscle relaxer, dry needling, nerve block injections, aerobic exercise, neuro-optometric adjustments, cranial- sacral therapy, and a significant amount of physical therapy.

Some things helped a little, but others not at all. I was slowly improving but would ultimately hit a plateau after each new treatment, and in time I exhausted all the standard protocols and had to look further afield for more answers. But before that happened, I hit my breaking point. And it was a doozy.

The Breaking Point

A year and a half into my recovery, I was back in Chicago living on my own, still working part time, and I began experiencing unusual physical and psychological changes. I couldn't sleep (at all), I had strange sensations of energy coursing through my body, my appetite increased, and I lost interest in eating meat. In addition, I had unusual heightened sensory experiences and experiences along the lines of what I imagine it's like taking psychedelics. Except I wasn't taking psychedelics. Friends and family began to take notice that I was speaking strangely, both in my cadence and the things I was talking about, and a few flagged that I sounded manic. Having no idea what mania was, I adamantly disagreed that any of it was a problem. I thought it was interesting and cool.

Then, on a Friday afternoon, I took a new migraine medication my neurologist had prescribed that week. It made me feel strange, and I wasn't sure if I should continue taking it. I also didn't know if it was safe to use with my medical marijuana, so I called my doctor's office and spoke to his nurse for guidance. It was late in the day, and she wasn't able to catch him before he went home. By the time he got my message on Monday, I was in the emergency room.

That Sunday night, I had felt myself oscillating between lucidity and confusion, waking up in the middle of the night after a few hours of sleep no longer in touch with reality (this experience could fill an entire book of its own). After a series of concerning texts and phone calls to friends, family, and my therapist, my people knew something was wrong and jumped into action. Two friends showed up at my doorstep, while a third was on her way. Meanwhile, my mom and sister were each booking flights in from out of state and had called 911 to send paramedics to my home. I was transported by ambulance to the nearest hospital, and a disastrous day was set into motion.

I lost consciousness in the ambulance and woke up in the emergency room with no idea who I was or what was happening. I had been taken to a small hospital without access to my records or medical history and was delirious and unable to communicate. Nobody knew I had a brain injury; nobody knew that I was taking a significant number of medications, or that I'd just had a strange reaction to a new one. My friends in the waiting room knew all of this and were trying to communicate it on my behalf, but the ER doctor dismissed or rejected the information they tried to supply. No one was allowed to be back with me, both because I was unable to give my consent and due to COVID restrictions. The doctor was a stone wall, no solutions were being offered or accepted, and it was a mess.

Complicating the situation further, due to privacy laws, my neurologist and his nurse would not speak to my sister, who was trying to alert them I was in the emergency room. She and my longtime work partner, who is also a close personal friend, spent an entire day on the phone trying to get the right people to talk to each other (or to them), while I spent the day alone, in and out of consciousness, in a state of panicked delirium.

I was afraid to close my eyes or lay down because I didn't think I would wake up again if I fell asleep, so I was heavily sedated. Each time I woke up, I was more confused, scared, and agitated at being alone, and would raise hell trying to get somebody to let me see the people I knew were in the waiting room. At one point I woke up to find myself tied to the bed with restraints. I did not know who I was or where I was, but I knew with certainty that I was in serious trouble and in the wrong place with the wrong people.

Knowing that the root problem was being overlooked, that the people with pertinent information were nowhere in my sight, that I could not communicate what I was experiencing, and being forcefully held down and drugged without consent was terrifying. The team at the hospital was doing the best they could, but it was a train wreck, and I was the train. After an intense daylong campaign by my people, my neurologist eventually had me transferred to his hospital so he could evaluate me. I spent the night and by the time he saw me the next day, I was presenting as completely normal. He sent me home to rest with instructions to follow up with him again at my next appointment in a few months. I was bewildered and exhausted, but lucid.

At home, I continued being unable to sleep, delirium set in again, and my pain spiked and became unmanageable. I saw colors. At one point, I felt like my forehead exploded from the pain. After a few days, I was taken to a different emergency room for a fresh evaluation by a new team of doctors, this time with my family along to advocate. On this visit, my pain was brought under control, and I passed both a psychological and a neurological evaluation. I was sent home again, with instructions to return if things got out of control again. They did within a few days, and we went back. Something was very wrong, but nobody could determine what.

I was eventually admitted to the hospital a second time to get to the bottom of what was going on. My mom and a dear friend were able to stay with me day and night to help keep me calm, while my body and brain were in complete chaos, and the situation was unwound. After a few days of monitoring and testing, it was ultimately determined that I was experiencing mania, either as a result of brain damage or most likely as an effect of the overlapping medications I was taking for symptom management. A significant number of medications had been layered over each other for a year and a half, prescribed by different doctors without coordination. It had all become too much for my body.

The mania was brought under control with medication, but it took months for my body to re-balance, and the entire calculus of my recovery had changed. After being released from the hospital, I was referred to a new network of specialists. Over the next year, the focus was on detoxing from my prior medications, finding new ways to manage the pain, revisiting physical therapy, starting speech therapy, and keeping the new concern for the possible recurrence of mania under control with carefully coordinated care. These things took close to a year to even out. During this time, I was utterly exhausted and in continuous pain, still barely able to maintain any aspects of a normal life. I finally stopped working to focus 100 percent on recovery because at this point, I no longer had a choice.

While this scenario is by no means typical for concussion recovery, it is indicative of how difficult it can be to manage and navigate a long and complicated process with many invisible factors and multiple medical providers across different medical systems. There can be unexpected symptoms, side effects, and complications that nobody sees coming. Also that you cannot get through recovery alone, and you will likely need to be your own persistent advocate.

I had the extreme privilege of love, support, and advocacy from my family and friends during this time, and there is no way I could have navigated this situation on my own. I will never forget sitting on my couch, dazed and delirious, while my sweet friend was simultaneously on the phone with my mother, answering the paramedics' questions and trying to gently stuff me into my boots and coat before helping me woozily navigate to the ambulance through a blizzard. Her deeply kind fiancé sat next to me, talking to me and keeping me calm. Friends and family ultimately escorted me to the hospital three different times that week, through three different snow storms, while ferociously navigating the medical system and banging down doors until we got the help that I needed. I am incredibly fortunate.

Fully Focused on Recovery

When I was hospitalized, a GoFundMe was started to help with medical bills, future treatments, and to give me a cushion for time away from work. The generosity people showed is one of the biggest blessings I have ever received. Sharing my story through this book is just one of the ways I hope to pay it forward.

After a few months of appointments and treatments in Chicago, working on getting my pain under control and recovering from the deep energy deficit the mania pushed my body into, I sold my home and moved to Des Moines, Iowa, to be near my family for support. I left ten years of friendships, a rock-solid career, and an amazing life behind. But at that point, I was so worn out that it didn't even feel like a tough choice. I had taken my hands off the wheel.

When I moved to Des Moines, things started speeding up for me. The reduced stress, time for rest, increased space, and loads of hands-on help from my family gave me the breathing room I needed to start coming back to life. It is also in Des Moines where I finally found the missing piece to my recovery: a very specific diagnosis of an injury in my neck (Cranio-cervical Instability, also known as CCI) that was causing my remaining symptoms and preventing full healing from taking place.

Working with a traditional physical therapist for manual neck therapy not only does not help someone with this diagnosis, it actually makes them worse, which is what happened for me. An atlas-orthogonal specialist (an upper cervical chiropractor) identified the issue and guided me through the treatment path, which at first was weekly adjustments at her chiropractic clinic and eventually a very specialized stem cell treatment to heal the damaged ligaments in my neck that were no longer holding the bones in place. This process took close to another year to work through, but it finally got me back on my feet and able to start the process of rebuilding my life.

Life Today

At the time of this writing, I have seen three primary care physicians, including one with a sports medicine background, one sports medicine specialist at a concussion clinic, two neurologists, eight physical therapists, a speech therapist, an acupuncturist, two physical medicine and rehab doctors, two therapists, a psychiatrist, a neuropsychiatrist, two neuropsychologists, an optometrist, a neuro-optometrist, a musculoskeletal specialist, an Atlas Orthogonal specialist and an interventional orthopedics specialist for the stem cell procedure. The persistence paid off.

I still experience daily pain and physical limitations, but I have been able to craft my life in a way that works for me and still allows healing to happen. There is no more pushing. These days there is flow, progress, and peace, and it feels like nothing short of a miracle. My story is not yet complete, yet I already consider it a happy ending.

Along with researching and writing this book and resuming part-time fundraising work, over the last year, I got certified as a holistic wellness coach so that I would be equipped to support others along their journey and hopefully even provide a few shortcuts. I work with more flexibility, less stress, and less anxiety, and I wouldn't trade my newfound passion and purpose for anything. Despite my continued symptoms, I have found joy again. I maintain the belief that as my neck continues to heal, my symptoms will continue diminishing and that I am on my way to an even fuller life. I get up every day excited to work toward my goals, even when the pain is high.

Whether you are reading this book to get a handle on which way is up, or to get the information you need to move forward through recovery with the confidence that you are doing it "right," or because you are in a deep, dark place like I was and are grasping for anything that might help pull you through, I hope you find it here.

As we move through the rest of these chapters, I encourage you to begin with the end in mind and believe deep in your soul in the strength of your body, and that you are recovering every single day. Take a minute now to close your eyes and think about what you want your life to look like on the other side of your recovery.

Allow yourself to really dream, even if it doesn't seem possible from where you are now. Get so clear on that image that it becomes part of you. Then let that image be the North

Star pulling you forward. Everything you do from here out is to bring you closer to that vision.

Be on the lookout for the pieces of information you can implement right now, today, to help you feel more empowered and in control to gain momentum toward your health and your vision.

Despite the messiness, remember that you are still in the driver's seat. Every injury and every recovery is different, but what is important to remember is how much we all have in common. We can do things to give ourselves and our bodies the fuel we need for the hard work of healing. Throughout the rest of the book, I will show you how.

I can't wait to celebrate progress with you on the other side.

PART ONE

Getting Clear

Chapter 1

Understanding Concussions

"You can't tough out a concussion."
—Jamie Huscroft

I did a lot of research during my recovery, looking to understand what was happening in my brain and body. As it turns out, it is not a particularly good time to study neuroscience when you're dealing with cognitive impairment and memory issues. This chapter synthesizes what I learned without going into the weeds on things like dendrites or neurotransmitters. These are the pieces of information that helped me wrap my (impaired) brain around why I was experiencing so much widespread physical chaos and what could be done about it. I hope that by understanding the chemical and physiological changes happening inside your body, you better understand what you are experiencing and that it is not "all in your head." You are also not alone.

The CDC estimates that as many as 3.8 million concussions occur in the US annually through sports and recreational activities alone.[1] From my understanding of that statistic, this does not account for falls, car accidents, concussions sustained during military service, or episodes of domestic violence, the prevalence of which is staggering.[2]

According to an article in *The New York Times Magazine*, research shows that abuse survivors can sustain head trauma more often than football players but are almost never diagnosed.[3] The most eye-popping statistic I've seen is from the non-profit organization Concussion Alliance, which shares that fifty-seven million concussions occur worldwide each year.[4] This is all to say that even though you may feel isolated during your recovery, you are far from alone and are, in fact, part of a silent epidemic.

Hearing the word concussion, or "mild" TBI, makes it easy to think it is less than a "real" TBI. However, I've seen it stated that, although concussion is the mildest form of TBI, it is the most complex. The Brain Injury Association of America addresses this by saying "The term *mild* refers to the severity of the trauma, not the consequences."[5] Dr. Kabran Chapek shares in his book *Concussion Rescue* that, "even mild brain injury can become chronic and cause long-term symptoms."[6]

A concussion is not just a bump on the head or a brain bruise. It is a true traumatic brain injury that causes very real and sometimes very long-lasting dysfunction. Throughout this chapter we will look at what exactly is happening inside the brain, what could be at the root of your symptoms, and an overview of what it takes to heal, even if you have been experiencing symptoms for years.

The Big Picture

A concussion happens when a jolt or blow to the head, or a hit to the body causes the brain to move back and forth inside the head at very high speed, bouncing, twisting, and/ or essentially ricocheting inside the skull. This results in brain cells getting stretched or damaged due to the force of the sudden and rapid acceleration/deceleration and is what sets off the chaos.

It is not necessary to lose consciousness to sustain a concussion. In fact, only about 5–10 percent of people do, and the initial severity of the injury, or whether you lose consciousness does not impact or predict the severity of symptoms or length of recovery.

A concussion does not cause structural or permanent damage to the brain. It is an injury at the cellular level that causes temporary dysfunction. The mass stretching of cells sets off an immediate, one-time electrical storm inside the brain with millions of neurons (brain cells) misfiring all at once. If you saw stars, this was that electrical storm. This initial cellular misfiring then causes a cascade of chemical changes in the brain that trickle down throughout the body and lead to the symptoms, dysfunction, and exhaustion we experience.

During recovery, the brain is rebalancing its chemicals and repairing any cellular damage. Research shows this process of rebalancing takes about 3-4 weeks. This takes a significant amount of energy and is part of why you may feel wiped out all the time and get tired more quickly after activities that used to be easy (I used to have to rest after taking a shower).

Because concussions do not cause structural damage to the brain, they do not appear on traditional imaging like x-rays, CT, or MRI scans. If your imaging was clear, it indicates there is not a more serious issue happening, like a brain bleed. It does not indicate that there is no cellular damage or dysfunction.

Currently, an assessment of symptoms and neurological performance is the only way to diagnose a concussion. However, new science is rapidly unfolding. Research is being done for biomarkers (i.e., blood and saliva tests) to indicate a concussion.

In addition to causing damage and dysfunction at the cellular level, concussions can also damage blood vessels, create problems with the gut and digestion, cause full or partial damage to the pituitary gland, cause inflammation across the brain and body, trigger visual, vestibular, and cardiovascular issues, and more.

Concussions can also trigger mental health changes and challenges. Dr. Daniel Amen, a leading TBI and brain health expert, states, "mild traumatic brain injury is a major cause of psychiatric problems, and very few people know it."[7]

An estimated 70–80 percent of people make a full recovery within a few weeks post-injury without needing any special intervention or rehabilitation.[8] New research is beginning to show that this number is high and that more people suffer from a longer recovery. For those whose symptoms persist past this window, there are underlying issues at play that need to be addressed with strategic interventions and/or rehabilitation. This is referred to as Persistent Concussion Symptoms (PCS) and was previously called Persistent Concussion Syndrome.

While it is not known exactly what causes PCS, Dr. Cameron Marshall, founder of Complete Concussion Management and a leader in the field of concussion education for both patients and medical providers, teaches that there are a number of physiological dysfunctions brought on by the injury that are thought to be the drivers of PCS. These are not things that heal on their own without treatment. Recognizing these underlying instigators and information on how to systematically address them is relatively new in the medical world and not yet common clinical practice. That is why it is often difficult to find well-informed and comprehensive care.

Here are the main theories Dr. Marshall shares that are thought to be the key drivers of PCS:

- Autonomic nervous system dysregulation (the body's ability to toggle between the fight-or-flight and rest-and-digest states we are meant to automatically alternate between) and blood flow abnormalities

- Inflammation and hormone dysregulation

- Visual and vestibular dysfunction

- Damage or dysfunction in the neck

- An overlap of psychological/mental health factors

Each of these things must be addressed strategically and systematically, and we will cover a streamlined framework at the end of this chapter.

First, we'll take a look at the specific symptoms you may be experiencing, which is the first step in identifying their underlying causes and your treatment path.

The Symptoms

The symptoms of a concussion are broken down into seven groups or subtypes, also known as phenotypes.[9] It is common to experience symptoms across many, if not all, categories. For some people, these symptoms will resolve on their own in a matter of days or weeks. For those whose symptoms don't resolve, they must be matched with the appropriate treatment programs and worked through accordingly.

Understanding which categories your symptoms fall into can help you delineate what you are experiencing into bite-sized pieces that you can address individually with proper treatment. As you go through this list, go ahead and circle or note which apply to you.

Cognitive

Symptoms include fatigue, decreased energy, headache, sleep disruption, difficulty concentrating, memory impairment, decreased attention and concentration, slowed mental processing speed, and other areas of executive dysfunction. (Executive function is our ability to problem solve, plan, focus attention, remember things, and juggle multiple tasks).

Vestibular

Symptoms include dizziness, fogginess, vertigo, balance problems, nausea, a feeling of being detached or "off", or overstimulation in noisy or crowded environments like stores or restaurants.

Oculomotor

Symptoms include headaches, fatigue, pressure behind the eyes, blurred or double vision, trouble focusing your eyes, your eyes not "keeping up" or tracking properly when you turn your head from side to side or follow an object, and light sensitivity.

Anxiety/Mood

Symptoms include anxiety, hypervigilance, increased irritability, feeling overwhelmed, sadness, and/or hopelessness.

Headache/Post-Traumatic Migraine

Headache is the most common symptom post-concussion, and it can follow several different patterns. Migraines, tension, cervicogenic (neck-related), and more are all possible and all treated differently. A concussion trained specialist can appropriately identify the type and guide your treatment path.

Cervical Spine (Neck)

Symptoms include headache, neck pain, dizziness, balance difficulties, or numbness and/or tingling of the extremities. Nerves, muscles, discs, and joints in the neck can all be impacted by the injury and contribute to neck pain, headaches, dizziness, and balance difficulties. These symptoms can easily be confused for visual or vestibular issues but are actually stemming from the neck. In fact, all concussions come with a side of whiplash, which mimics PCS symptoms. Many people with prolonged symptoms who do not get better with treatment have an underlying neck issue that has not yet been properly addressed. This was the case for me.

Cardiovascular

Symptoms include exercise intolerance, heart rate changes, lightheadedness, autonomic nervous system dysregulation (getting stuck in fight or flight mode), elevated heart rate, and others.

Sleep

Sleep is not a formal category, but I want to flag that it is very commonly impacted after a concussion. Many people experience drowsiness, a need for excessive sleep, difficulty falling asleep, altered sleep patterns, and/or waking from sleep feeling drained vs. refreshed. In many cases sleep requires medical support to address.

Not all symptoms appear immediately. The chemical changes in the brain create a cascading effect that can cause the symptoms you experience to change and/or develop over time. As a result, you may notice additional symptoms popping up hours, days, or even months after your injury. Being familiar with the full gamut of symptoms that may arise will help you to be able to recognize them as related to your injury and that they are treatable.

For me, sadness, irritability, and a decreased tolerance for stress were big symptoms that I had no idea were related to my injury. I recognized that I was significantly more irritable, but I thought this was a standard reaction to the chaos and pain I was living with. I did not realize it was a physiological result of the injury. I also noticed that I always felt better on the weekends (even in the early months when I wasn't working), when I wasn't worried about what work obligations were piling up, or wondering if my phone would ring with requests. I recognized the correlation but never considered it something that I actually could or needed to address. If something impacts your symptoms, make a note of it and discuss it with your team to find solutions. Our bodies are always giving us signals and clues for where to go next for progress and relief.

I experienced almost every symptom on the list severely for more than a year, many for more than three years before

I found the right treatment providers for my individual issues and started making significant improvement. If you are reading this book to understand someone going through recovery, try to imagine living with any number of the above symptoms, around the clock, with no idea when things will get better. It feels like being stuck underneath a dark, heavy blanket. It's physically and emotionally painful, exhausting, and scary in there.

But the good news is that all these symptoms can be treated, even if you have been experiencing them for years.

The Solution

After twenty-four to forty-eight hours of cognitive and physical rest immediately after the injury and ruling out any serious medical issues, it is recommended to begin gradually returning to activity both physically and cognitively. The key is to only resume activities up to the point that does not make your symptoms significantly worse (a little bit worse is ok, the goal is to gradually increase your tolerance). This is not a case of resting until you feel better, although rest is also an important component of recovery. An early graduated return to activity is what improves recovery time.

It used to be recommended to begin seeking specialized care and treatment around two weeks post-injury, but new research is showing that pursuing rehab as early as a few days after the injury can be beneficial. Recovery requires strategic active rehabilitation paired with your individual symptoms, adequate rest, and not doing too much too soon. You must strike the right balance and work through the appropriate protocols for your specific symptoms gradually.

During recovery, it is absolutely critical to avoid a second impact to your head until you are fully healed. A second impact can worsen recovery outcomes and even cause permanent damage, and in rare cases can be life threatening.

Healing persistent concussion symptoms is a lot like peeling away the layers of an onion. You need to address the outer layers before moving deeper. In my opinion, the most straightforward way to do this is to begin working through the layers with the following steps. Although the framework is simple, each of these steps is nuanced and often complex. You'll find more information, tools and strategies for each throughout the remainder of this book.

1. **Seek treatment:** Identify your symptoms and begin plugging into the appropriate medical providers and rehabilitation programs for your needs. This step takes a while. In the meantime, begin working your way through the rest of this list. As you move along and monitor progress, continue exploring deeper and deeper layers of symptoms and treatments as needed.

2. **Address your sleep dysfunction:** The body needs sleep in order to heal. If you're not sleeping, you're not healing. You must be proactive about addressing this.

3. **Optimize your nutrition:** Proper nutrition will give your body the nutrients it needs to heal, support reduced

inflammation, and help heal any gut issues that may be causing your symptoms. It is common for the gut lining to become dysfunctional after a concussion, and this is often a key symptom driver. The link between the gut and the brain is so significant that the gut is often referred to as the second brain.

4. **Strategically exercise:** I know this may sound terrible right now, but it is an integral part of the recovery process. Exercise addresses many underlying issues, including autonomic nervous system dysregulation. If your symptoms worsen with exercise, a strategic exercise program is actually the prescribed treatment.

5. **Manage your mindset:** Managing your mindset can help reduce your symptoms. In my opinion, this is a significantly overlooked and underrated component of recovery.

6. **Seek mental health care:** Mental health challenges can be brought on by, and/or exacerbated by the injury and can prolong recovery, not to mention that recovery in itself is stressful and anxiety inducing. In some cases, symptoms that appear as cognitive dysfunction are actually caused by mental health factors. It's a piece that must be addressed with proper support.

7. **Learn how to pace yourself:** Pacing is about learning how to function on a day-to-day basis within your window of tolerance without doing too much too soon.

8. **Regulate your nervous system:** If your nervous system is out of balance and stuck in fight-or-flight mode, as is almost always the case after a concussion, it will induce symptoms and get in the way of healing. Multiple things earlier on the list will have already addressed nervous system regulation, but it will still need to be monitored and supported with additional tools.

9. **Seek support:** Recovery is hard, and is not something you are meant to do on your own. Ask for the help and support you need, both logistically and emotionally.

10. **Keep the faith**: Recovery is a process and progress does not happen overnight. Keep faith in yourself and your body, believe that you are healing, keep doing the work, and continue peeling away the layers of the onion until you reach the other side.

Once you've identified how you will address all the above, you've got to do the work and stick with it. This is hard stuff. Throughout the rest of this book, you will find more information, tools, and strategies for implementing each of the steps. Remind yourself that these things take time, and you are not expected to address them all at once. You will also never get any of it perfect. Give yourself grace and permission to take it all one step at a time.

Now that you have an idea of what is happening inside your body and a step-by-step process to follow to promote healing, in the next chapter, we will dive deeper into what to expect during the recovery process. If you're feeling bamboozled by this strange world you've found yourself in, this one's for you.

KEY TAKEAWAYS

- ✓ Concussions have a wide-ranging effect across the body. They do not cause structural damage and do not show up on standard imaging like MRIs or CT scans. The dysfunction they cause is temporary.

- ✓ After a day or two of complete rest, it is time to get moving again within your window of tolerance. This means leaning into some discomfort, but not pushing so hard that your symptoms significantly increase.

- ✓ For people who do not recover on their own after a few weeks, recovery requires a strategic, progressive, active rehabilitation program with specialized medical providers based on your individual symptoms.

- ✓ It is absolutely critical to avoid a second impact while you are still healing.

- ✓ A full recovery is possible even if you have been experiencing symptoms for years.

✓ To help you navigate the steps listed above, download the free bonus workbook at www. theconcussioncompanion.com/freebonus

Chapter 2

Recovery 101

"You can only see as far as the headlights,
but you can make the whole trip that way."
–E.L. Doctorow

During the first two years of my recovery, there were days when I would be lying in my bed with my eye mask on, feeling overwhelmed, confused, and hopeless. I remember wishing there was a book that I could leave open to a specific page that would just tell me what I needed to know. I was craving validation and answers. Specifically, I wanted to know if I was doing something wrong, if I was missing something, and if recovery was this hard for other people too. I wanted to be reminded of the answers every single day. In case you are feeling this way too, I created this chapter as an introduction and overview of the big picture of recovery that you can turn to for reminders whenever you need them. The rest of the chapters moving forward will be much more tactical, but these are the things I think it's helpful to know right

The Concussion Companion

up front. These are the big picture reminders and validators that I was craving.

In many ways, my own recovery felt like an example of how *not* to do recovery. I made major missteps from the outset due to lack of knowledge. I did not rest in the first few days. I did not use a gradual return-to-activity or return-to-work approach. I did not back off when my symptoms increased. I did not find my way to the right providers until it was way past time. Then again, it also feels like the progression of my recovery is a common one.

It is common to experience:

- confusion about guidelines and protocols.

- difficulty navigating return to work.

- difficulty finding the right providers.

- plateaus or regressions in progress.

- insurance and financial factors standing in the way of specialized treatments and providers.

- stress, fear, and anxiety that complicate the whole situation.

But, there is good news. Even if you missed the boat on finding the right providers or following the right protocol at the beginning, like I did, it's not too late to get on track and make progress.

A foundational aspect of recovery is managing your expectations and mindset, so you don't get frustrated when things aren't moving quickly or as you expected them to. Frustration creates stress and tension, which leads to increased symptoms. It's also important to be aware that there are things that could slow down healing or hold it back.

Let's start by getting clear on what you are working with, including that recovery is a choose-your-own-adventure type of deal. Your doctor(s) likely won't have all the answers, and some may give you outdated or misinformation, or straight up blow you off and dismiss your symptoms. You will need to be proactive and be your own advocate to find the care and support that you need, and you may very well kiss some frogs along the way.

Also, and this is a big one, recovery is not linear. Your symptoms may change from day to day, week to week, and month to month. In my own recovery, I could feel the very slow and steady underlying improvement from month to month but was always caught off guard by the severe symptom flares when they hit—especially the mood swings, panic attacks, irritability, and depression. It was easy to understand why I was in pain or dizzy, but the psychological symptoms were difficult to come to terms with, particularly when they seemed to come out of nowhere. Know that things shift and change, and this is a natural part of the process. Your job is to go slow, pay attention to your symptoms and triggers, and adjust your activity level and treatments accordingly.

Below are eight recovery realities that are important to keep in mind.

Recovery Realities

1. Recovery requires patience.
Recovery takes time, and nobody can tell you how long. It could be days, months, or years. There is no one correct path to follow. You may double back on treatments and providers, and you will most certainly spend time waiting on the medical system or for progress to present itself. This can be endlessly frustrating. Remind yourself that the need for patience is simply how it goes, and that pushing, stressing, or fuming will only make things worse.

2. Progress is not linear.
If only I had a dollar for every time I've heard this! It was easy to understand rationally, but so hard to accept when setbacks happened. It still is. You may be doing well and making marked progress one day, week, or month, and then have a major flare-up or setback the next. You never know exactly where you are in the recovery process, and surprises (the bad kind) can and often do pop up. I often thought of recovery as a game of chutes and ladders. When I unexpectedly fell down a chute, I would try to remind myself that a ladder was undoubtedly ahead; I just needed to keep myself moving forward until I got there.

3. Your doctor may not have all the answers.

This was the hardest truth for me to accept. I wanted my doctors to be able to tell me exactly what to do next, how to handle getting through between appointments, and where to go for answers and information. But due to the nature of the injury, the lack of concussion education within the medical community, and the limited time doctors have to spend with each patient, it just doesn't work like that. You will likely have to do your own homework, be a strong advocate for yourself, and count on tools and resources from outside your doctor's office to support you.

I also had to learn that doctors are people too. They each practice through the lens of their own expertise, opinions, and personal experiences. And just like all people, some are more open minded and compassionate than others. It may take multiple providers or multiple opinions to find the right fit for you.

4. Simple things may now be hard.

Things that you took for granted, previously simple, may be difficult and painful now. Some will feel downright impossible. Most days, I was too fatigued to shower. On days that I actually did shower, I would have to lay down in my towel to rest immediately afterward. Loading or unloading the dishwasher flared my headaches and made me dizzy and nauseous to the point that I had to lay down. Sorting laundry was too hard for my brain; I would hold the clothes and be unable to figure out which pile they were supposed to go in. Sometimes

I looked at a website and couldn't comprehend how to navigate it or where to click. I couldn't follow a multi-step task, like following a recipe. Making a grocery list was too overwhelming. Making a phone call was daunting and draining. Going into a store was an absolute nonstarter. These things are not just hard; they are taxing for your brain and drain your already limited energy. You are not making it up.

5. Mental health impacts everything.

Physical pain can impact your mood, and your mood can impact your physical pain. It's cyclical. Addressing the emotional challenges associated with (and often as a direct result of) the injury is not something to put on the back burner. Supporting your mental health is an important piece of the puzzle that will positively impact your physical health and symptom progression.

6. The body stores trauma.

Our bodies hold on to trauma, even if our conscious minds don't remind us of it. Trauma associated with the circumstances of your injury, or PTSD, or previous instances of trauma in your life can affect you silently from the inside out. It can manifest as physical pain, anxiety, sleep trouble, and other physical symptoms that impact recovery. If stored trauma is impacting your symptoms and healing, things like physical therapy won't solve the problem. Addressing the trauma with a mental health professional may be a necessary step for unlocking another level of recovery. You may need to do very deep work.

7. Conventional wisdom does not always apply.

I find that many times recovery is at odds with conventional wisdom. We need to have the presence of mind to separate what is good for us from what is good for everyone else. Advice like "fake it 'til you make it" and "no pain, no gain" will not serve you here.

8. Mindset matters.

Our bodies respond to our thoughts, both positive and negative. This has been scientifically proven. You can use your mindset to fuel your recovery and help pull you forward or let it drag you down and hold you back. I will spend an entire chapter on this later in the book (see Chapter 7).

I'll be honest, *knowing* these things didn't exactly make dealing with them easier, but it helped manage my frustration by understanding that everyone else was dealing with the same realities. I encourage you to come back to this list when you are feeling frustrated to remind yourself that what you are doing is difficult and complex, and that just because it's hard does not mean you are doing it wrong.

Now that we've acknowledged the reality of what we're working with, next we will get into more specifics of the big-picture recovery process.

Your Recovery Team

Your team will likely be multi-disciplinary, and following your symptoms is the path to putting it together. Depending on your symptoms and the length of your recovery, your team may change over time. In the first three years of my recovery, I worked with close to thirty different providers. Partially because I received care in two different states, but mostly because one person would take me as far as they could, and then release me or pass me off to the next when they didn't have anything further to offer. This was exhausting, exasperating, and as it turns out, not all that uncommon.

Try to keep the perspective that each provider you see brings a different piece of the puzzle to the table. Treatments will run their course. One provider may take you as far as they can, and then it's time to re-evaluate. As I've mentioned before, moving through the stages of recovery is a lot like peeling an onion. You'll keep coming to new layers that require different approaches. Throughout this process, keep your faith in yourself, your persistence, and your resilience, not in what any one provider has to say or offer.

Fuel for Your Body

Your body is doing hard work right now. It requires the right fuel and environment in order to support the recovery process. This means good sleep, sufficient hydration, proper nutrition, and exercise. All these things felt impossible for me at first, but that didn't change that they were important factors that needed to be addressed. They are what sets your body up for healing and also support pain reduction. We will get into the specifics in Chapters 5 and 6.

Pain Management

I was four months into my recovery before a new doctor explained that my job was not just to endure the pain, trucking along biting on a stick until things got better. This was news to me. I thought I just needed to hang on and suck it up.

After acknowledging that concussions are a big hot mess, really overwhelming and difficult to navigate, he explained that pain management helps healing to occur. This was reiterated to me again later by my neurologist.

Basically, when the body is in pain, everything is out of whack. Things need to calm down in order to get back into whack. It's our job to help facilitate the process so that our body can divert more energy to healing, and it likely *will* be a process. It won't happen overnight, and your pain most likely will not completely disappear, but it does need to be addressed to give your body at least a bit of relief.

The following is a basic overview of the most traditional modalities for pain management.

Medication

Many medication options are available to help with pain management and other concussion symptoms, including headaches, nausea, sleep impairment, mental health challenges, and dizziness. Medication is a short-term solution while your body heals and/or you are pursuing therapeutic treatments. While they can absolutely help, they do not address the root causes of your symptoms and will not get you better on their own. They can serve as a bridge while you are working through your treatment program.

While medication can be an important piece of the puzzle, it's also important to be aware of the potential side effects. For example, if you use over the counter pain medication daily for an extended period of time, you are at risk for rebound headaches. This happens when the body is used to getting a certain medication every day and actually creates headaches on its own if it doesn't get its daily dose. I experienced this and can attest that the headaches were very real and very severe. I couldn't tell they were "rebound" and not "natural." It took about a week of clearing my body of these medications before the rebound headaches subsided. Be sure to pay attention and monitor any side-effects you may experience.

In my own recovery, it took experimenting with a lot of different things over a long period of time. Many things helped some, but not enough, but we kept at it. I tried every combination of over-the-counter pain relievers, many different prescription medications known to help alleviate migraines, muscle relaxers, trigger point injections, nerve block injections, and topical pain relievers in addition to things like physical therapy, dry needling, and acupuncture along with myofascial release and craniosacral therapy. I also used medical marijuana. Ultimately, it was my work with the atlas orthogonal chiropractor and the stem cell procedure that brought things under control. Now I only work with a physical therapist on myofascial release for the remaining neck pain and headaches, and meditation and breathwork are all that I need on a daily basis so long as I don't push past my limits.

Natural Options

There are also many natural approaches to pain management, including acupuncture, mindfulness, meditation, massage, heat and ice, breathwork, magnesium soaks, tai chi, and much more. Cognitive behavioral therapy, a type of talk therapy, has also been proven to help with pain management. I will admit that I blew off most of these methods as ridiculous at first, until I discovered for myself that they actually do make a difference. It is a matter of experimenting to find what works for you.

I relied heavily on meditation, and now I find that I can meditate my way *out* of some headaches. Diaphragmatic breathing also makes a difference for me. Mindfulness, meditation and breathwork all help regulate the nervous system and have additional recovery benefits, including helping with mood, anxiety, and depression and calming your body and mind when they are in overdrive. All of this can lead to reduced pain. I will cover meditation and breathwork in more detail in Chapter 7.

Physical Therapy & Rehabilitation Exercises

I want to include physical therapy and rehabilitation exercises here because they are long term solutions for pain management. Don't be afraid if your treatments increase your pain in the short term. This is what they are supposed to do. It is how you get to the root of your symptoms and progress your way back to baseline. Using medication or the natural options listed above can be tools to support you while you are working through your rehab program.

Blocks to Recovery

In addition to doing the right foundational things to support your recovery, it's also important to address any factors that may be slowing you down or straight up blocking your progress. Major contributors that can hinder your recovery are lack of sleep and/or exercise, pushing too hard, stress, mental health factors, and inflammatory foods like gluten, dairy, sugar, and alcohol. If you are feeling like a deer in headlights at the thought of addressing these things right now, know that they can be addressed over time and taken one by one as you feel ready and able. For now, just take in the big picture ideas.

Stress

It's easy to gloss over stress as an intangible factor in our overall health, but it's not. Stress is physically damaging to the brain and can increase pain and hinder healing. It triggers the release of cortisol, which triggers biological functions that negatively impact brain function. High levels of cortisol can also kill neurons in the brain's memory center, which results in an inability to think clearly. Over time, your brain can actually be rewired (for the worse) by stress. Stress also negatively impacts sleep, which is a foundational need for recovery, and can trigger and contribute to pain. The hitch is, of course, that recovery is incredibly stressful. Finding tools to diffuse and manage it is critically important and should not be overlooked. Working with a mental health professional and using mindset tools can both be helpful.

Lifestyle

It's also important to look at lifestyle factors. Habits and routines that served you well without a brain injury may not serve you right now. One of the greatest surprises to me was how much I had to overhaul many of my norms and automatic behaviors in order to progress. At times, I felt like I was being mercilessly served challenge after challenge to unwind every single unhealthy habit, thought pattern, or way of being in my life in order to move to the next stage of recovery.

The anxiety I'd lived with for most of my life could no longer go unaddressed. The depression that used to come and go intermittently now needed attention. Lack of intentional sleep habits no longer cut it. I couldn't hold up to the stress and demands of my job. I had to learn to say "no," and hold boundaries, even when it upset other people. Perfectionism meant that I pushed too hard and made things worse. I had to learn to be kind to, and gentle with myself, which I had previously believed was a surefire way to become soft and lazy and waste my life away.

These things took a *lot* of self-education and therapy to work through, and are things I don't think I ever would have addressed had I not felt their direct correlation to my pain and symptom levels. In the end, this work led me to a happier, healthier place than I was at even before my injury, but it was no joke to work through.

Consider the following lifestyle factors. Could any of them be impacting your recovery?

- Stress

- Nutrition

- Sleep

- Exercise

- Alcohol consumption

- Sugar consumption

- Relationships

- Thought patterns (Are you consistently hard on yourself?)

- Personality (Are you a type-A person who likes to push and achieve?)

- Mental health and trauma (Is there trauma associated with your injury that needs to be addressed, or do you have previous traumas that are stirred up by the mental health challenges of recovery?)

These are big and may feel overwhelming at first. There are no right or wrong, good or bad answers; they are simply things to consider. Self-awareness is key. Start by paying attention to the things in your life that you may be doing on autopilot and see if there is anything you may need to adjust or address for recovery. Don't worry yet about what you're going to do about it. Just start by identifying what you think could use some work. We'll get more into the "how" later.

Meet Yourself Where You Are

Everything in recovery must start with meeting yourself exactly where you are. Accept and honor that you can only do so much at a time right now. You cannot give what you do not have. You may need to start with baby steps. If all you can manage is cereal for dinner (this was me for a long time) or you're struggling to get out of bed, that's where you are. You are not lazy or weak. That's just where you are in that moment, and it's okay.

We all come to recovery from different places and have different obligations to manage. You may be able to keep working or not. You may have a choice or not. You may have a family to take care of or not. You may be surrounded by a wonderful community or not. You may have access to good medical care close by or not. These are all factors in your recovery that require you to acknowledge where you're at to identify your path forward.

It might not be as easy as just "finding the right doctor." You may need to ask someone to help you do the research and make the calls. You may not be able to make a major diet overhaul right now. That's okay. Maybe you start by adding in a few baby carrots with breakfast to increase your vegetable intake; it doesn't have to be fancy. If you're feeling depressed and like everything is too hard, look to low-hanging fruit resources like *Psychology Today* or *Better Help* to get matched with a therapist quickly, possibly without even leaving your house. Identify the most important thing right now, whatever the biggest block to progress is, and take the next tiny step to move yourself forward. Trust that with a few more tiny steps, you'll build some momentum, and progress will unfold.

As we move forward through the rest of the book, I simply want you to keep in mind that the way forward is to take the next step, big or small, one at a time. You are not meant to digest and implement all this at once. Start by taking it in and feel for what seems like the next step for you to take from wherever you are now.

Now that we have gone over the big picture of recovery, we will cover exactly how to navigate the maze of medical providers in the next chapter.

KEY TAKEAWAYS

✓ Recovery is messy. This doesn't mean you are doing it wrong.

✓ Unless your symptoms resolve on their own in the first few weeks, you will likely need to put in work and effort in order to actively promote recovery.

✓ You may need to make some lifestyle adjustments to either support your body's healing or remove roadblocks to it.

✓ Nutrition, hydration, sleep, exercise, mental health, and stress management all play key roles in recovery.

✓ Pain management is important. Be sure you are addressing this with your doctor. It may take time and experimentation.

✓ The work of recovery can be daunting. If you need to, choose one piece at a time to focus on. You can identify and work on your biggest hurdle first, or start small and build momentum.

Chapter 3
Navigating the Medical World

"You are the CEO of your own health."
—*Tony Robbins*

I still remember the first time I sat across from a doctor who I felt truly understood what I was going through and knew the right steps forward. I was four months into my recovery and had been referred to a doctor within my family practice clinic who had experience in sports medicine. I walked in with a long list of questions, and for the first time, I didn't have to ask any of them. Instead, he knew exactly what to ask *me*. I felt like I had been carrying around a heavy backpack, and somebody took the weight off my shoulders for the very first time.

In case you haven't had the opportunity to meet with a provider like this yet, let me sum up what he said to me. It went something like this:

"Concussions are a really hard thing. You're in pain all the time; you're exhausted, but you're not sleeping. A million things are going wrong, and it could take any number of treatments to get things fixed, and we have no idea what's going to work. Your symptoms change all the time, and it's exhausting to be running around to appointments constantly, and it's basically just a big mess. There's no right way to do this, so I'm really just here to help you navigate this and be your cheerleader along the way." *Yes! That's it!*

It was so validating to hear this spoken by a doctor. After this, I started referring to him as my "cheerleader doctor," and what he brought to the table for me was priceless.

I left that appointment feeling good about my action plan for the first time since my injury. We agreed that we needed to go back to basics and start at the beginning. First, we needed to get my pain and sleep under control in order for anything else to improve. This was eye-opening to me because, until that point, both pain and sleep impairment had been so out-of-control that it didn't seem in the realm of possibility that they could actually be improved.

We started small, with over-the-counter and topical pain relievers. They didn't move the needle a ton, but it was a start. We also experimented and ended up using a combination of muscle relaxers and a heavy dose of Benadryl to get me sleeping at night, which was not ideal, but it worked. And that's what I needed to get me moving forward.

We also agreed that it was time for me to switch physical therapists. Until then, I had been working with a holistic physical therapist doing primarily cranial sacral work, which was slowly benefitting my headaches but was not addressing my most pressing functional impairments like visual and vestibular issues. I made a change and began working with a concussion trained vestibular physical therapist who worked with me on a strategic rehabilitation program to address my headaches, dizziness and eye strain, and also performed manual work on my neck. This started moving the needle more quickly for me, and I knew I was finally on the right track.

Finding clear and compassionate guidance like this is easier said than done. I experienced my recovery while living in a major US city and still found it difficult to navigate the system and find the right providers. You may not find someone who makes you feel like they've taken the heavy backpack off your shoulders, but it is possible to find that support and validation elsewhere (I'll cover some good options for this). What you need is someone who can help guide you through finding the right specialists, remain as your touch point along the way to help monitor progress, and make adjustments as needed. If you can't find someone knowledgeable, you can also do the research on your own and check in with your doctor as needed.

Working with knowledgeable providers is key. That said, there is no one clear path for recovery and no singular treatment program that works for everybody. That is why understanding the treatments available for your specific symptoms is essential to help you know if you are on the right path. This chapter outlines the most common concussion treatment modalities, specialists, and resources for finding them.

Where to Start & When to Pivot

After getting cleared by a medical doctor that you do not have any severe underlying damage, if your symptoms have persisted for longer than a week or two, it's time to start getting plugged into specialized care. New research is showing that it's not too early to start this process even earlier.

Working with a family practice doctor/primary care provider familiar with concussion management or a sports medicine doctor is a good place to start getting plugged into specialty care. Many people get referred to a neurologist early on as well, which can absolutely be a good thing, but not all neurologists are trained in concussion care. This is something to be mindful of. Know that within every specialty, sports medicine and neurology included, there are varying degrees of knowledge on concussion management. It is vitally important to find doctors and providers who are experienced with concussion treatment. If your primary care provider is unable to give you a good referral, go ahead and do some research on your own. Seeking a second opinion and asking questions based on your own knowledge to identify if they are the right fit for your needs may be necessary.

I thought I was in good hands with my first neurologist until I met with my second neurologist. Then I realized I'd sunk six months into the wrong provider. It was gutting. Remember, if you're not getting results, change it up, and don't be afraid to seek more than one opinion.

Getting plugged in with a knowledgeable medical doctor is an important first step, but it is only the first step. They will likely serve mainly as a touchstone. You will also need to put together a team of providers who will support you with symptom-specific rehabilitation and treatments. Finding the right providers requires research and legwork on your part. This is how it goes. Take the time to call the clinic or provider you're considering, to confirm they have substantial experience treating long-term concussion symptoms, and that they don't just list the word concussion on their website. Some of the best referrals I received were from word of mouth from people who had dealt with a concussion themselves, many of them through a friend of a friend. I encourage you to post on social media that you are seeking help navigating concussion recovery to see if anyone in your world knows someone in your area with experience. Ask your friends and family to post about it too. Getting results requires casting a large net but may pay off handsomely. I also include a few provider locators later on in this chapter.

Concussion Clinics

These specialty clinics cover all the rehabilitative specialties required to address concussion symptoms all under one roof. They do an in-depth intake assessment covering your medical history and injury, and develop a comprehensive treatment program that they will manage in-house with coordinated care. Different clinics run the range from offering basic rehabilitation programs, to much more comprehensive and cutting edge.

There are also a number of specialized treatment centers across the US and Canada that work with patients who travel in for short-term, intensive treatments if you are unable to find a good clinic in your area or are not making progress. These specialized programs tend to be the most comprehensive and cutting edge.

Building Your Own Team

If you do not have access to a concussion clinic, you can go the DIY route and put together your own team. This is what I did.

As we've discussed before, different treatment options are utilized for treating different symptoms and you will likely need to put together a multi-disciplinary team. The sooner you start, the better.

Below are the most common types of specialists who treat concussion symptoms:

Physical therapists (PTs)

Physical therapy is usually the most common place to start. PTs can treat many of the common symptoms of concussion, including exercise intolerance, vision and vestibular issues, balance, and neck dysfunction. Try to find a concussion trained PT if you can. A good way to identify if a PT clinic is up to speed on concussion management is to call and ask if they do the Buffalo Treadmill Test at their clinic. Different PTs have different areas of expertise, so don't get discouraged if you need to work with more than one over time.

Speech therapists/speech-language pathologists (SLPs)

SLPs are trained to help navigate cognitive, communication, and executive function challenges.

Neuro-optometry and vision therapists

These specialists treat vision disturbances and oculomotor issues, including difficulty reading, trouble retaining written information (this is often thought to be a cognitive problem but can actually be from vision issues), difficulty driving, and difficulty with screens. Occupational therapists and physical therapists with vision training can also help, but complex cases will require more specialized support from neuro-optometry or a specialized vision therapist.

Vestibular therapists & ENTs

Vestibular therapists treat symptoms including dizziness, feeling "off", and balance issues. There are regularly trained vestibular therapists as well as concussion trained vestibular therapists. See if you can find one who is concussion trained as they will be more specialized. ENTs treat vertigo, balance issues, and ringing in the ears.

Chiropractors, osteopaths, and upper cervical chiropractors (Atlas Orthogonal or NUCCA)

All can be seen to address neck issues, including neck pain, reduced range of motion, headaches and dizziness. I know many people, me included, who found significant relief from headaches and other symptoms after getting treated by an upper cervical chiropractor and wish this specialty was more well known.

Mental health professionals (psychiatrists, neuropsychiatrists, psychologists, neuropsychologists, and therapists)

Irritability, anxiety, depression, PTSD, and cognitive impairment can all be addressed with mental health support from a psychiatrist, psychologist and/or therapist. Neuropsychologists can perform an initial assessment of cognitive and emotional symptoms and guide your treatment path.

Functional medicine doctors and naturopaths

Functional medicine and naturopathic doctors can help with holistic aspects of recovery, including diet and supplements. Depending on their training and specialty, some providers are also able to address more broad ranging aspects of recovery. They can be an excellent addition to a recovery program as a whole.

Endocrinologists

Endocrinologists diagnose and treat hormone dysregulation.

Occupational therapists (OTs)

OTs can help with navigating cognitive challenges and supporting you with getting back to daily activities and work. This type of support tends to be more functional in nature, not typically addressing the root causes of dysfunction in a rehabilitative way, but focusing on strategies for reintegrating into regular life.

Functional neurology

Many people have experienced good results working with a functional neurologist when other medical treatments have not helped. Treatment methods vary, and they use a multidisciplinary approach to identify and address the root causes of persistent symptoms, including headaches, visual and vestibular issues, cognitive dysfunction, and more.

You most likely will not need to work with all these specialists. Start by identifying which providers treat the symptoms you are experiencing, then see who you can find in your area who is specifically trained in concussion management and rehabilitation. Start by lining up one or two, then expand as you progress and rule things out. Keep in mind that addressing your diet, sleep, and exercise will also play an important part in reducing your symptoms too.

This list covers the most common treatment approaches. For additional and alternative options, I recommend *The Concussion Repair Manual* by Dr. Dan Engel. His book covers a wide range of options for complementary and alternative therapies and is a wonderful resource if you want to do a deeper dive. These likely will not replace more traditional modalities but can be great to explore to see what might feel good for you in addition to your current program.

It's worth another reminder here that what different doctors and specialists offer you will vary. Each provider has their own lane, experience, and beliefs about what works and what doesn't. One person may have more knowledge of concussions and experience than the next. It may take some time to find the right people for your needs, but never consider that you are out of options. Keep going until you land in the right spot. If or when you hit a ceiling with one provider, keep your head up and move on to the next.

Headaches

I also want to spend a little extra time on headaches. They are noted as the most common and often the longest-lasting symptom of concussion, and they need to be treated correctly. Most concussion patients report post-traumatic headaches that, in some cases, linger for months or years.[10]

It's common to get referred to a neurologist who will prescribe medication for migraines, but it's also important to be looking for and addressing any root causes that are not migraine related. There are a number of different types of headaches that all need to be treated differently, including neck related and tension headaches. Headaches can also be caused by visual issues, stress, or nerve damage, and it is possible to have multiple different types of headaches layered over each other. Identifying your specific headache types and/or causes with your medical providers is important and may be a case of needing to peel back the layers of the onion one at a time.

Provider Locators

The Brain Injury Association of America, Complete Concussion Management (great for folks in Canada), and the Concussion Legacy Foundation (CLF) all offer free resources to get you pointed in the direction of knowledgeable providers. Many other online locators are available, but I have found these to be the most comprehensive. The Concussion Legacy Foundation also offers a helpline staffed by volunteers who will answer questions and help you find the right resources for your situation.

Although it is not a service listed on their website, my local chapter of the Brain Injury Association of America also matched me with a patient advocate who provided referrals to recommended providers in my area. I recommend making a call to your state office to see how they can help.

Provider Locators:

- Brain Injury Association of America

- CLF Concussion Clinic Finder

- Complete Concussion Management Clinic Finder

- CLF Concussion Helpline

There are also online resources to help connect you with mental health providers, including virtually, if you are struggling to find someone in your area, or want to connect with a therapist without having to leave your home. Here are a few good places to start:

Mental Health Provider Locators:

- Psychology Today can help you find providers in your area, including those who work on a sliding fee scale.

- Better Help offers online virtual counseling.

Online Education Programs

If you are struggling to find a knowledgeable specialist to guide your rehabilitation program or a supportive community, I highly recommend getting plugged into an online program like Concussion Fix, Concussion Compass (at the time of writing this program is on pause, but check their website for updates), or The Concussion Community. Utilizing one of these online programs will ensure you are getting the most robust and up-to-date information to be your own advocate and find your way to the right providers for your needs. They will educate and guide you on work you can be doing at home between your appointments, and they can also help save you time and money that would otherwise be spent pursuing the wrong treatments at the wrong time with the wrong people.

If you can't handle the screen time, dispatch a friend or family member to help with this. When I first joined Concussion Compass, I didn't utilize it because it was too overwhelming for me to even log into the program dashboard. Once I got started, I listened to the videos with my eyes closed or my eye mask on. Make it work for you. Again, I encourage you to ask a friend or family member to help you with this if you are stuck. There is so much good information out there if you can access it.

Programs to consider:

The Concussion Community

Based in the Netherlands, founded by Silvie van de Ree after her own recovery struggle. This monthly membership program includes live group coaching from a TBI coach, a wide-ranging roster of classes and courses led by experts, a library of resources to help yourself from home, a private podcast for members, and a private online support community.

The Concussion Fix

This program was founded by Dr. Cameron Marshall, Sports Specialist Chiropractor and founder of Complete Concussion Management. It offers in-depth teaching videos with best practices for recovery, weekly live group calls with concussion-focused healthcare practitioners, recommendations for proper interventions, and tools and resources for taking actionable steps.

Concussion Compass

Although this program is on pause, there are plans for it to return and I don't want to skip over mentioning it because it is fantastic. Co-founded and run by Dr. Molly Parker, a physical therapist who is in long-term recovery herself, Concussion Compass is a monthly membership program offering education and mentorship from experts. The program offers mini courses taking you through the lifestyle, mindset, and rehab topics that are foundational to concussion recovery, as well as self-assessments to help understand the root cause of your symptoms, exercises, and tools to help you make changes from home. It also features guest experts and a supportive online community. Check their website for updates on the program's re-opening.

Throughout the last three chapters, we have gone over the big picture of recovery, how it works, and who can help. But in addition to finding the right therapies and treatment providers for your individual needs, there is important work to be done every single day at home, *between* your appointments. In the coming section, we will cover exactly what you can do on a day-to-day basis to give your body the fuel it needs to recover.

KEY TAKEAWAYS

✓ Start by identifying a knowledgeable primary care provider, neurologist, or sports medicine doctor who can refer you to the proper specialists for rehabilitation or seek out a concussion clinic.

✓ If you are struggling to get good referrals or to find a concussion clinic, put together your own team of specialists based on your symptoms.

✓ Utilize online provider locators to get connected with specialists in your area.

✓ Consider getting plugged in with an online education program for further support.

PART TWO

Essentials for Healing

Chapter 4

Hydration, Sleep, and Movement

"You can't build a great building on a weak foundation."
—Gordon B. Hinckley

You know that feeling of desperation you feel between appointments? When you're lost and alone and don't know what you're supposed to do every day for the next three or six months before seeing your doctor again, and you just want to cry? Take a deep breath and focus on the basics: hydration, sleep, movement, and nutrition. I call these things the essentials for healing. They are critical to setting your body up for success in the recovery process and are important to focus in on here because they take work, discipline and diligence to do well. This is some of the most important work you can do to support your body's healing.

Our country has a lifestyle epidemic. It's accepted as the standard way of living to be overstressed, undernourished (nutritionally, relationally, emotionally, spiritually), and exhausted. This is just the way it is, we think. It must be this way for everybody. And we're not wrong. According to the CDC, only 6 percent of Americans engage in what are considered the top five healthy behaviors:[11] maintaining a healthy weight, not smoking, not drinking excessively, getting enough physical activity, and getting enough sleep.

Living by this standard does not set you up for success in the healing process. The foundational aspects of health and wellness that are so easy to ignore or take for granted in normal times must become priorities during recovery. Your body needs adequate water, sleep, exercise, and the proper nutrients in order to heal. These are not ideals; they are necessities.

If you are open to it, one of the silver linings of recovery can be the forced focus on health and wellbeing, even if it comes about in an undesirable way. The aspects of health that need to be addressed to support recovery will also give you a solid foundation for long-term wellness post-recovery, too. My own goal was to come out of my recovery healthier, stronger, and happier than I went in. I went so far as to type out this mantra and tape it up on a wall in my apartment. I walked past it countless times a day as I did my physical therapy exercises and always kept it in the back of my mind to help pull me forward.

I found that focusing on practical, measurable things like hydration, sleep and movement was helpful not only for physiological reasons, but psychological ones too. There are so many choices to make during recovery. Not the least is, "How am I going to make it through another day like this?" I found that focusing on a small list of things I could control gave me a sense of purpose and some ownership. Without having something to focus on, I was toggling between flailing and languishing, completely at the mercy of my symptoms every day. At the same time, it also felt like being stuck in quicksand. But if I was working on my sleep practice, checking off "fully hydrate" and "go for a walk" from my to-do list, or meeting a nutrition goal, I felt like I was doing something that would slow the sinking and eventually help reverse it. Just to be clear, this did not make the situation feel easy. But it did give me a sense of empowerment and control.

For a long while, I made my priority hydration because, in the days of the worst pain and emotional symptoms, this was something I could actually do. *My goal today is to drink this whole pitcher of water.* That's it. I was still languishing, but I was also doing something.

Throughout the day, when I would start spiraling into negativity and the emotional red zone, asking, "What am I even DOING right now?" the answer would be: *I am hydrating. Go get a glass of water.* Pivoting back into alignment with my goal and taking action that I knew would support my body's functioning and healing could usually slow the spiral. As things progressed, I was able to increase my goals and feel a much more significant sense of accomplishment with what I was doing each day. This work continues for me now, and my priorities shift and change with time. Yours will too.

Let's do a deeper dive into the recovery essentials now. As we move forward, don't worry about implementing all of this at once, simply pick and choose what feels like the next right thing for you to focus on as you go.

Hydration

We all know that hydration is important, but raise your hand if you actually fully hydrate every day. That's what I thought. I know I didn't before my injury, and it turns out I am not alone. It's estimated that 75 percent of Americans are chronically dehydrated.[12]

There are two reasons I'm starting with hydration first. The first is that it's foundational to our body's functioning. The body and brain are both made up of 70 percent water.[13] We need water to function. It forms the building blocks of our cells, and without it, our cells become sluggish and struggle to perform their functions optimally. During recovery, this is extra important because your cells are working overtime to heal your body. Additionally, water moves nutrients throughout the body, which is also vital to our recovery. And in my opinion, hydration is also the easiest thing on this list to focus on and accomplish when you can't do much else. If you are really struggling right now, start here and work your way up.

A few more points on the functional importance of hydration:

- After a concussion, the body's blood-brain barrier is often compromised. This is an inner control mechanism for keeping toxins out of the blood stream. When things get into the blood stream that aren't supposed to be there, it creates inflammation and dysfunction that impacts our symptoms. Water helps flush this stuff out.

- If any brain cells have died as a result of the injury, it creates *extra* toxins that need to be cleared out.

- Hydration impacts energy levels and brain function.

- Dehydration can trigger headaches.

- Drinking enough water helps us sleep better, improves mood and concentration, and helps with cognition.

Important things here, yes? But to get these benefits, you need to be drinking *enough* water. A good goal is to drink half your body weight in ounces daily. So, if you weigh 200 pounds, you drink 100 ounces each day. If you weigh 100 pounds, you drink 50 ounces daily, etc.

For a long time, finishing my water each day was my only goal. It was all I could handle, and it gave me a goal I could actually achieve. If you are in a place where nothing feels possible, start by focusing on hydration and use the sense of accomplishment to build momentum toward bigger goals.

Tips for Hydration

- Get a large pitcher that measures out your daily ounces goal. Refill it every morning. Use it to refill your glass or water bottle throughout the day. Set a goal that you can't go to bed without finishing it.

- Get yourself a dedicated water bottle that you take with you all day, every day. Do the math to figure out how many refills you need to drink each day to hit your daily ounces goal. I have one that only requires one refill and it works great.

- Find a water bottle that has the hours of the day marked on the side. This is a good visual reminder to help you see if you're on track with your water intake or not. These are easy to find on Amazon.

- Set a reminder to go off on your phone every hour, or every few hours, with a reminder to hydrate. Then drink a glass of water.

- If you are someone who does not like the taste of water, try adding slices of fresh fruit for flavor. I like to use lemons, limes, oranges, and cucumbers.

Sleep

Your doctor will likely ask you how you're sleeping, and if you're like me, you will blow this off. Who cares how I'm sleeping? You get as much sleep as you get, and that's that, right? Not in recovery. The importance of sleep and what it does for our bodies is incredibly heightened after a brain injury. Not only does it rest and recharge our bodies and minds for the day ahead, but it's also when our bodies do their repair and healing work. During sleep, the body is clearing out toxins and repairing damaged tissue, and after an injury there is more work to do than usual.

Every system in the body, especially the brain, is impacted by the quality and amount of sleep we get. Things like our ability to cope with stress, our mood, our immune system, inflammation, metabolism, sugar cravings, and brain circuitry are all affected by sleep. Poor sleep can increase anxiety and chronic pain and contribute to stress. Sleep deficits can also contribute to long-term health risks, including obesity, diabetes, dementia and Alzheimer's, cancer, and an overall shortened life expectancy.

There is also a link between sleep deprivation and increased inflammation in the body.[14] Since inflammation is one of the biggest battles we're fighting against, this is critical. Adequate sleep also contributes to neuroplasticity, which is the brain's ability to change and heal itself. Reducing inflammation and supporting neuroplasticity are two of the primary goals during recovery.

Put simply, the brain needs sleep to recover from a TBI. Not getting enough sleep can worsen many symptoms, including fatigue, mental confusion, pain, depression, anxiety, mood swings, and memory problems. Some people's need for increased sleep lasts for an extended period of time, if not permanently, after a brain injury. It's not uncommon for people to need ten hours of sleep per night post-injury. For the first three years I needed eleven to twelve, and then I was able to taper down to nine, but I had to follow my body's lead on this.

The challenge, of course, is that sleep is massively impacted for the worse by a brain injury. I had trouble falling asleep and staying asleep for close to three years after my injury, which prolonged my body's ability to heal. So, what do you do?

The most common ways to address sleep issues start with sharpening up personal sleep habits and routines. This struck me as annoying and futile at first (the term "sleep hygiene" makes me cringe), but the truth is there is a lot of science behind the recommended practices, and they are worth attempting. According to the book *Brain Wash* by David Perlmutter, M.D. and Austin Perlmutter, M.D, "good sleep hygiene will likely outperform everything else in the long term."[15]

Good sleep habits include going to bed and getting up at the same time every day, limiting naps, minimizing caffeine intake, not eating within 3 hours of going to bed, limiting exposure to screens and bright lights an hour or two before bed, having a consistent wind-down routine that signals to your body it's time to get ready for sleep, and getting early morning sunlight outdoors. Getting even 10 minutes of direct sunlight in the morning can help wake you up and improve your circadian rhythm, the body's natural sleep-wake cycle.

Caffeine, alcohol, and sugar can all negatively impact sleep and reducing or eliminating them for a period of time may be necessary. For me, all three majorly affect my sleep quality for the worse and this became hyper-present during recovery.

Once these initial sleep habits have been established (or attempted), next steps may include a sleep study, natural sleep aids like supplements and herbs, followed by medication if necessary. Therapy can also be helpful. Stress, anxiety, and pain can all negatively impact sleep, which is why working with a therapist can be helpful. Some therapists even specialize in insomnia.

Sleep inducing medications can have significant negative side effects, including fatigue and brain fog, which, for obvious reasons, are not ideal during recovery. That's why it's important to address sleep habits first, along with any work you can do with a therapist and/or trying natural options, to avoid medication if you can. That said, medication may be necessary in order for you to move forward. I relied on various medications for more than two years before I was able to get my sleep stabilized. I didn't like this, but my doctor helped me understand that without sleep happening, recovery wasn't happening, so I bit the bullet. Now that I no longer use these medications, I can see how much my sleep habits affect the quality and quantity of sleep I get. I must stick to my routine in order to keep things on track. This takes discipline, but it's worth it.

The bottom line is, getting sleep during recovery can feel impossibly difficult. But it matters significantly, both now and in the long run, and must be made a priority. If you are sleeping a lot and still feeling fatigued and foggy, discuss this with your doctor; you could be suffering from low-quality sleep, which means you are not spending enough time in the deep stages of sleep where healing occurs. If this is the case for you, a sleep study or working with a psychologist or counselor who focuses on insomnia may be a necessary next step. The personal sleep practices mentioned earlier can also have an effect on sleep quality. It is all a big circle, and addressing your sleep habits is a good place to start.

While you are working through all this, if you can't sleep, think about how you can *rest*. This can help pivot your mindset away from frustration and move you into a space of relaxation where your body and mind can still rest even if you aren't sleeping. Meditation, breathwork, progressive relaxation, and Yoga Nidra can all be helpful with this. Yoga Nidra is a guided meditation practice that helps you enter a deep state of relaxation, calms the nervous system, and can give you some of the benefits of sleep without you actually entering the sleep state. It is said that a 30-minute Yoga Nidra practice is equivalent to 2-4 hours of sleep.

For more information on helpful sleep habits and natural approaches to improving your sleep, I highly recommend the book *Sleep Smarter* by Shawn Stevenson. Each chapter of the book details a different strategy, tool, or tip ranging from the somewhat obvious to the somewhat out there. Many of the suggestions overlap with other fundamentals of recovery, so you may find some ideas for force multipliers. It's also an enjoyable read, and Shawn shares his own story of recovery from a significant injury. For audiobook lovers, he narrates it and his voice is lovely. I highly recommend it.

Tips for Sleep

- Develop a consistent evening routine to signal to your body that it's time to prepare for sleep.

- Try to go to bed at the same time every night so that your body gets into a rhythm. (A consistent wake time is important too, but I found that I felt best when I let myself sleep for as long as possible without an alarm.)

- Get at least 10 minutes of direct sunlight in the morning.

- Try to finish eating 2-3 hours before bed.

- Minimize exposure to screens and bright lights in the evening, especially 1-2 hours before bedtime.

- Experiment with eliminating or reducing caffeine, alcohol, and sugar intake.

- Keep your phone out of your bedroom, or at least away from your bed.

- If you are awake for more than 20 minutes at a time during the night, get out of bed and move to a different environment until you are sleepy again.

- For additional information, including tips on supplements and additional natural tools and practices to support healthy sleep, check out *Sleep Smarter* by Shawn Stevenson.

Movement

We all know that exercise is necessary for a healthy life, but for me, exercise felt impossible during recovery. I needed to readjust my expectations for what exercise looked like, and ultimately replacing the word *exercise* with the word *movement* helped me set my sights on something more attainable.

Movement is medicine for recovery. Not optional medicine. Foundational medicine. It directly addresses one of the common underlying drivers of persistent concussion symptoms, which is blood flow issues, and supports sleep, mental health, and mood. However, exercise intolerance is common post-concussion, and there is a really delicate balance that must be struck here. This was a tough one for me to work through, and the most helpful motivator for me was understanding the science behind why it's so important. If you're struggling to understand the power of movement for recovery, or to motivate yourself to get moving when you feel like absolute garbage, consider the following:

Mild exercise or gentle movement (we're talking about going for a walk, not going to a HIIT class) produces chemicals that the brain needs to heal as well as addresses underlying blood flow issues and autonomic nervous system dysregulation, which can be key contributors to PCS. Even if movement worsens your symptoms, it is still a critical component of recovery. In fact, if this is the case, slowly and gradually increasing your tolerance is the treatment protocol. Avoiding it can prolong recovery time, and the longer you go without it, the worse your symptoms can become.

Movement increases blood flow to the brain, which brings the oxygen it needs, improves brain function, memory and cognition, increases energy, helps control inflammation, and works as an overall repair kit for damaged brain cells (hello! Sign me up). It also rewires the brain for better functioning and can help reduce the symptoms of depression. Worthwhile, right? Keep these benefits in mind when you need something to pull you forward.

Be sure to discuss with your treatment providers the exact exercise parameters they recommend based on your current ability level and symptoms. How much? How often? What kind? The general recommendation is to do something that keeps your heart rate elevated but steady (something aerobic, not interval training or weightlifting) and does not significantly increase your symptoms. It will increase your symptoms some, and this is the goal. My neurologist told me that I must exercise, but didn't give me the details, and I ended up pushing too hard for a full three months before seeing him again and discovering that I was doing it wrong and causing myself a significant amount of unnecessary pain and exhaustion. I was so deflated after that appointment I ended up in tears.

It is ideal to work with a trained concussion specialist or physical therapist to establish your program and parameters. They can do simple treadmill testing called the Buffalo Concussion Treadmill Test to precisely establish a specific protocol for you and monitor your progress. If you don't have access to this type of provider, there are also ways you can do this on your own.

Depending on your pre-injury lifestyle, it may be equally difficult for you to either dial down your movement routine or dial it up. I fell somewhere in between. If you're struggling with symptoms that get in the way of what you consider to be exercise, remember that the goal is *movement*. Exercise does not need to be vigorous to be beneficial. The goal is daily mild aerobic exercise that increases your heart rate without significantly increasing your symptoms (a general rule of thumb is note where your pain level is on a pain scale of 1-10 before you begin, and try not to let it increase more than two to three points). If you do too much and your symptoms increase exponentially, back off the next day. Keep experimenting until you find your sweet spot.

Before my injury, I was a periodic runner. Now due to my neck injury, I can only tolerate walking, and even that was difficult for the first few years. This felt like a major fall from grace and was difficult to accept. In the early days, I started walking around the block once a day, as often as possible. Being outside in bright sunlight was painful, and my dizziness made walking challenging. I moved very slowly. Eventually, I could do a 20-25-minute walk each day under the guidance of my physical therapy team with heart rate and careful symptom monitoring. My goal was to gradually increase the speed and duration of my walks. I'm still doing this work now.

Rather than get upset, I opted to find humor in my further exercise attempts. The first time I tried a HIIT workout, I sat down on the floor and cried afterward because I was so overstimulated. And then I laughed because it all felt so ridiculous. Doing any sort of aerobic or strength exercises that required coordination were also comical. Moving an arm and a leg simultaneously in opposite directions was something my brain simply couldn't process. If I did pull it off, I often fell over due to balance issues and again would just laugh. These things provided me with good benchmarks for celebrating progress though. When my brain could finally process the mechanics of doing a lunge, it was huge!

In addition to aerobic activity, additional forms of gentle movement like yoga and stretching can be beneficial for balancing the autonomic nervous system, reducing pain, and supporting sleep. Due to the nature of poses like twists and inversions, typical yoga studio classes likely won't be a fit with your symptoms, but there are wonderful programs designed specifically for people with TBIs, as well as accessible yoga and chair yoga that can be done online from home. The Love Your Brain Foundation offers yoga designed for people with TBIs, as does Amy Zellmer, founder of Faces of TBI. I also love Yoga with Adriene's free YouTube yoga videos. If you are working with a teacher in person or virtually, be sure tell them about your injury and what movements you may need to avoid. If you do some exploring to find a teacher whose style resonates with you, you may even find a wonderful home and healing community to move through recovery with.

When it comes to movement, don't discount whatever it is you can do to start. I've read that even getting up to walk around your house for two minutes once an hour is enough movement to benefit you. Start somewhere, and you will be able to build over time gradually. If you can tolerate more vigorous exercise, be sure to pay attention to any symptom increases and discuss them with your medical provider.

Just like with building new sleep habits, I know it can feel exceptionally difficult to make yourself do the work when you don't notice any immediate benefits. Remind yourself of what movement and exercise are doing for your brain and try to consider it one of your medicines.

Tips for Movement

- The general goal is to increase your heart rate without significantly increasing your symptoms. Start small and work your way up, even if this means starting with walking just a few minutes each day.

- Remember that if your symptoms increase with exercise, the treatment protocol is exercise. Discuss the details and your symptoms with your doctor or physical therapist, especially if you are dealing with heart rate anomalies. Their guidance is very important.

- Find a friend or family member to go on walks with you and to stay accountable to.

- Experiment with gentle online yoga programs you can do from home. Here are a few to check out:
  - ✓ The Love Your Brain Foundation
  - ✓ Amy Zellmer (search for her videos on YouTube)
  - ✓ Yoga with Adriene (search for her "gentle yoga" or "restorative yoga" videos on YouTube).

In addition to hydration, sleep and movement, high quality, brain healthy nutrition is also essential for recovery. We will dig into this in the next chapter.

KEY TAKEAWAYS

✓ Hydration, sleep, and movement are essential for helping the body fuel its recovery.

✓ When it feels like there is nothing you can control, focus on the things you *can* control.

✓ If you need to, start small. Choose one area to focus on and one action you will take each day.

✓ Developing new habits takes time. Celebrate your wins and honor your commitment to your health and your recovery. You are doing big work!

Chapter 5

Nutrition

"Food is medicine."
—Origin unknown

For a long while in my recovery, I relied on friends and family to both pick up my groceries and keep me fed. My boss gifted me with a meal kit delivery service that was a godsend, but also usually too difficult for me to prepare so I had people help with that, too. Once I got past the point of having consistent support, there were many days when the best I could do was cereal for dinner. At that stage of the game, making nutritional changes was nowhere near feasible. I was in survival mode.

But as I progressed, I made little changes. I switched to oatmeal instead of boxed cereal. I incorporated smoothies when I could. And when I began preparing meals again, I kept them very simple, focused on whole, non-processed foods as much as I could and did my best to eat a lot of vegetables. Keeping it simple like this actually checked a lot of the "nutrition for recovery" boxes and gave me a solid foundation to build on.

I understand how difficult it can be to incorporate big changes when you are in survival mode. If that is where you are right now, let this chapter give you an idea of what you can work toward as you are able. Also, keep an eye out for simple tricks that you can incorporate right now. Boosting your nutrition doesn't always have to be complicated.

Nutrition plays key role in recovery. It is one of the primary tools for addressing chronic inflammation, which is a potential driver of PCS and many of the symptoms we experience. Most people don't know it's common for the gut lining to become dysfunctional after a concussion, which causes inflammation and other symptoms, and the treatment for this is to heal the gut using supportive nutrition. Headaches, fatigue, brain fog, nausea, anxiety, and depression can all be triggered by issues in the gut that need to be healed with dietary adjustments. Diet also impacts neuroplasticity, the brain's ability to heal itself.

Giving our bodies the nutrients required for brain health and healing, and removing the things that can be holding us back is foundational to paving the way for healing to occur. Depending on what your diet looks like currently, this may be an area that you need to address with gusto or one that just requires a few tweaks. I want to make clear that when I say diet, I mean a general way of eating, not a weight loss program.

Consider the idea that food is medicine. The food you put into your body either directly supports and fuels your energy, clarity, and healing, or it harms it. When it comes to nutrition for recovery, an anti-inflammatory diet is the general goal. We want to increase nutrient-dense whole foods and healthy fats such as olive oil, avocado oil, coconut oil, avocados, nuts, and seeds along with high-quality proteins, while eliminating or reducing processed foods, sugar, and, depending on your personal needs, possibly gluten and dairy. These are the goals. But like everything else, you've got to meet yourself where you are. Starting with small changes is okay.

Because different approaches to nutrition work for different people and different bodies, I will outline a few options here. Pursue whatever feels good and manageable to you. I encourage you to gain an understanding of the key principles of these diets and apply the pieces that work for you. If making a major overhaul or going cold turkey doesn't work for you right now, give yourself breathing room to simply make the best choices you can on any given day and make progressive changes over time.

The Whole Foods Approach

The most straightforward dietary change you can make to support recovery is switching to a whole foods diet. This will support reducing the inflammation that occurs after a concussion by reducing your intake of inflammatory foods and increasing those that fight inflammation.

"Whole foods" simply means foods that are not processed. When you're looking at an item in the store, ask yourself if nature made that food or if a factory made that food. In addition to whole foods being nutritionally dense, by eating a whole foods diet, you are automatically eliminating the refined sugar, processed carbohydrates, trans fats, and many of the inflammatory ingredients found in processed foods. Switching away from processed foods and moving toward a whole foods diet checks a lot of boxes.

If the thought of eliminating processed foods feels terrifying or impossible, start by focusing on what whole foods you can add to your diet rather than on what you will cut out. Prioritize fruits and vegetables, especially dark leafy greens, and foods that are high in fiber like gluten free whole grains, and healthy fats. Make a list of the foods you would like to add in and post it on your fridge. Add something green to every meal, like a handful of snap peas, sliced cucumbers, or green peppers. A good rule of thumb is to aim to fill half your plate with vegetables. Begin by adding things in and let your new food choices start to crowd out the old.

Reducing or eliminating refined sugar is also important to recovery, and this will basically take care of itself once you make the whole foods shift. Dr. Engel refers to sugar as one of the worst things you can expose yourself to during your TBI recovery. Sugar consumption promotes chronic inflammation, negatively affects mood and cognitive function, negatively impacts sleep, and forms free radicals in the brain, which can damage cells and cause further dysfunction.

Eliminating gluten and dairy for a brief period (30–60 days) may also be necessary for many people as an additional step. This will support the healing of the gut lining and blood-brain barrier, both of which often become dysfunctional after a concussion. When these internal control systems malfunction, toxins and inflammatory substances that should not be getting into your bloodstream and traveling to your brain are able to sneak through the lining in your gut through small micro-tears, causing inflammation. The gut lining and blood-brain barrier can both be healed, and the first step is removing inflammatory foods. The biggest perpetrators are gluten and dairy. Eliminating them for a period of time will allow the gut lining to heal, and also allow for your nutritionally dense foods to better do their job of fueling your body and recovery. You may also wish to explore this further by incorporating prebiotic and probiotic rich foods, and/or supplements into your diet.

Antioxidants

Whole, nutritionally dense foods contain antioxidants that are not present in processed foods. Antioxidants are natural substances such as vitamins, minerals, and other food compounds that are believed to fight free radicals in the body (free radicals form when the body undergoes stress, e.g., after an injury, and can cause damage to cells).[16] In the case of recovery, antioxidants also contain the essential nutrients our bodies need to repair, heal, and provide optimal brain function.

As you make your food choices, focus on choosing foods rich in antioxidants to best fuel your recovery and brain function, and as an added benefit they will also help to prevent disease in the long term.

Antioxidant-rich foods include berries, cruciferous vegetables (broccoli, kale, and brussels sprouts are a few examples), spinach, herbs, orange vegetables (carrots, sweet potatoes and squash, etc.) nuts and seeds (pecans, walnuts, hazelnuts, and sunflower seeds), garlic, and green tea. A good way to get more of these foods into your diet is by incorporating them as snacks, or as simple sides with meals.

Antioxidant-Rich Foods:

- Berries
- Citrus fruits
- Broccoli
- Kale
- Brussels sprouts
- Spinach
- Bell peppers
- Tomatoes
- Avocados

- Herbs
- Carrots
- Sweet potatoes
- Squash
- Nuts and seeds (e.g., pecans, walnuts, hazelnuts, and sunflower seeds)
- Garlic
- Green tea

It's also important to eat a wide variety of different colored fruits and vegetables, or to "eat the rainbow". This is a good way to ensure you are getting a wide variety of different vitamins, minerals, and antioxidants as the different color families of foods contain different nutrients. Try to change things up from time to time, rotating your go-to fruits and vegetables so that you are covering all the bases.

Food Quality

The most foundational step is to eat primarily whole, nutritionally dense foods, but quality matters too.

Studies have shown organically grown food to be more nutritionally dense than conventionally grown food. For example, organically grown foods are higher in antioxidants. Conventionally grown foods are also higher in harmful chemicals that can cause inflammation and a number of other symptoms. This applies across the board to fruits, vegetables, grains, meat, fish, and dairy.

Upgrading to organic food can be expensive. A good place to start is by utilizing the Dirty Dozen list, which gives you the top twelve foods it is recommended to switch from conventional to organic.[17] These are the foods that contain the most chemicals from pesticides and where you'll get the most bang for your buck when making the switch. The same organization also produces a Clean Fifteen list, telling you which foods are safe to buy conventionally grown. For instance, it is recommended to switch things like berries, spinach, kale, apples, and grapes to organically grown, while avocados, onions, asparagus, mushrooms, and cantaloupe are safe to continue buying conventionally. New lists come out every year; simply do a google search for "Dirty Dozen and Clean Fifteen" to see the latest. I keep these lists posted on my fridge.

These lists focus on produce, but upgrading the quality of your meat, fish, eggs, and dairy if you are eating it, also brings significant nutritional benefits. Grass-fed and pasture-raised meats are higher in nutrients due to what they are fed (you are eating everything the animal eats—if they are raised on food high in nutrients, those benefits are passed on to you. If they are raised on low-quality feed, like conventionally raised meat, those inflammatory properties are also passed on to you). Grass-fed meat is also higher in beneficial fats. The same principles apply to fish, eggs, and dairy. Conventionally raised are less nutritionally dense and higher in antibiotics, while dairy and eggs from organic, pasture-raised, grass-fed sources, and wild-caught fish are significantly higher in the nutrients your body needs for recovery.

The labeling on all these things can be confusing. Look for organic grass-fed or pasture raised meats, wild-caught fish, and organic, pasture-raised, Certified Humane or Animal Welfare Approved eggs certified by a third-party organization.

It is not in my budget to purchase all my produce, meat, fish, and dairy this way, so I do the best I can. I slowly integrated more of these things into my diet over time and have now modified my diet to eat less meat and less dairy, but a higher quality of both. I only purchase the highest quality eggs and only wild-caught fish, as well as grass fed meat as often as I can. This was a process for me, and over time I found ways to offset the higher cost of high-quality proteins with some of my other food choices. Just like with everything else, meet yourself where you are and start where you can.

The Keto & Paleo Diets

If you are already eating a high-quality, whole foods diet and are interested in making further refinements to supercharge your body and brain's functioning, there are several diets recommended for optimal brain health and their anti-inflammatory benefits.

The Keto Diet can have powerful benefits for the brain and is sometimes referenced as the ideal diet for recovery, but the reality is that it's not realistic for many people. The Keto Diet switches your body from burning sugar as its fuel source to burning fat, which leads to longer lasting energy and increased brain function and healing. It's a very technical diet that involves counting macronutrients (fats, proteins, and carbs) and sticking to a strict regimen. If you feel that switching to a keto diet may be a fit for you, discuss it with your doctor. It is very important to do this in conjunction with a medical professional as it can cause side-effects and is not safe for some people with underlying medical conditions.

In *The Concussion Repair Manual*, Dr. Engel suggests one option to make this diet more attainable is to take "a more ketogenic dietary approach" which means leaning more heavily towards eating healthy fats, and sticking to a moderate protein intake and relatively few carbohydrates. These changes alone can go a long way toward providing your brain with what it needs to repair itself.[18] Basically, follow the guiding principles of the diet without focusing on the counting

A secondary option is to go Paleo, or more Paleo, a diet that is high in lean proteins, healthy fats, fruits, vegetables, nuts, and seeds, and avoids refined sugar, dairy, grains, and legumes. I went this route in my own recovery and found it to be an easy-to-follow framework. Over time, I discovered that my body feels better when I am eating some gluten free whole grains rather than eliminating them, and have brought them back into my diet. As with all things, it's important to listen to your body and do what feels good for you. I enjoy the *Against All Grain* series of cookbooks by Danielle Walker as a Paleo resource. Her books include education on the parameters and how to stock your kitchen for success, sample meal plans, and are basically an over-all Paleo resource hub. I have cooked primarily from her cookbooks for quite a while and love them all.

Making changes in the direction of either of these diets will automatically move you away from the processed foods, refined carbohydrates, unhealthy fats, and sugars that cause inflammation and make a mess of things in the brain and the gut.

I also recommend the book *How to Feed a Brain* by Cavin Balaster if you'd like to go deeper on the subject of nutrition for recovery. This is one of the most impactful books I read during my own recovery and impacts many of the food decisions I make today. Cavin is a survivor of a severe traumatic brain injury and researched in depth the specific food groups and nutrients needed to fuel brain recovery and long-term brain health and function.[19] The book goes into detail on specific foods to focus on adding into your diet, including prebiotic and probiotic-rich foods, and it gives a straightforward framework to follow.

Keep in mind that it is not necessary to stress yourself out by going all in on any diet. It is okay to begin by taking small steps in the right direction and make the choices that work for you.

Vitamins & Supplements

Vitamins and supplements can also be an important part of making sure you are getting adequate amounts of the nutrients you need, especially if there are any areas where you are deficient. This topic needs to be addressed with a doctor, as needs vary from person to person and need to be checked with blood testing. Some of the key nutrients the body needs in order to support healing are omega 3s, vitamins B, D, and E, magnesium, zinc, and iron. Traditional medical doctors can run basic lab tests for some deficiencies such as vitamins B and D, and functional medicine doctors and naturopaths can do a deeper dive into nutrients that traditional doctors aren't equipped to test for.

In addition to vitamins to support any deficiencies, the most commonly prescribed supplements for TBI recovery are fish oil, magnesium, and curcumin. If you would like more resources on supplements, Dr. Chapek provides a detailed overview of the benefits of different supplements and includes a sample regimen in his book, *Concussion Rescue.*

Be sure to look for high quality vitamins and supplements. Unfortunately, many contain low quality ingredients and fillers and don't carry as many benefits as they claim.

Sample Meals

To take some of the guesswork out for you, here are a few of my favorite no-cook and low- cook meal options that meet the nutritionally dense, high in healthy fat, anti-inflammatory diet criteria:

Breakfast:

- Fried or scrambled eggs with fruit and veggie sticks.

- Fried or scrambled eggs with avocado slices and salsa.

- Egg cups packed with veggies (mushrooms, spinach, onions, garlic, zucchini, etc.).

- Mixed green salad with blueberries or orange slices, avocado, hard-boiled egg, and Primal Kitchen balsamic vinaigrette (Primal Kitchen is my go-to brand for Paleo friendly condiments).

- Smoothie with almond milk, water or coconut water, spinach, kale, cucumber, fresh ginger, and an apple, frozen banana, or frozen pineapple for sweetness. I keep the fruit to a minimum with the priority on packing in the greens.

Lunch:

- Tuna salad with Primal Kitchen mayo and sliced fruit and vegetables.

- Mixed green salad with leftover grilled salmon or chicken, veggies, and vinaigrette.

- Sliced deli meat with veggies and avocado.

- Dinner leftovers.

Dinner:

- Lettuce cup tacos with avocado and sliced bell peppers.

- Spaghetti with meat sauce and zucchini or spaghetti squash noodles.

  Note: Rao's makes an excellent clean marinara sauce, and Green Giant makes frozen zoodles that require only a microwave to prepare. Spaghetti squash can also be microwaved and then scraped into noodles with a fork. I rely on my microwave a lot to keep meals "low-cook".

- Baked salmon with microwaved sweet potatoes and broccoli, or frozen vegetables.

  Note: pierce the sweet potato with a fork a number of times and cover it with a wet paper towel. Microwave for 5 minutes, turn it over, and microwave for another 4–5 minutes. For the broccoli, add a small bit of water to a bowl with the florets and microwave for 3–4 minutes.

- One of my dinner tricks is to lean on raw vegetable slices as sides. Not only do they not require cooking, but they are higher in fiber than cooked vegetables.

We have covered a lot here. The key thing to remember is to increase your intake of whole, nutritionally dense foods and eliminate or decrease processed foods, gluten, dairy, and sugar. Make changes slowly if you need to. As you know, stress is the enemy of recovery, so if it's between stressing out over having a little sugar in your salad dressing vs. being proud that you're eating a salad choose the celebration. Do what you can do and be ok with making changes over time. If you start by cleaning up the basics, you will be setting up a strong foundation.

In addition to hydration, sleep, movement and nutrition, there is one more essential for healing. In the next chapter, we'll dive deeper into how to harness the power of mindset to support your recovery.

KEY TAKEAWAYS

✓ Commit to adding whole, nutritionally dense foods high in antioxidants to your diet.

✓ Eliminate or reduce processed foods, gluten, dairy, and refined sugar from your diet.

✓ Refer to the most current Dirty Dozen and Clean Fifteen lists when choosing which produce to purchase organic.

✓ Upgrade the quality of your meats, fish, eggs, and dairy as it works for you and your budget.

✓ Set yourself up for success. Keep sliced vegetables on hand. Clean out or set aside the products that do not support your recovery. Make a list of the foods you would like to increase and post them on your fridge as a reminder when it comes time to make the grocery list.

- ✓ Use your microwave—sweet potatoes, broccoli, spaghetti squash, and frozen vegetables all microwave well.

- ✓ For a deeper dive into nutritional recommendations, check out How to Feed a Brain by Cavin Balaster.

- ✓ For more details on recommended supplements, refer *to Concussion Rescue* by Dr. Kabran Chapek.

Chapter 6

Managing Your Mindset

"Whether you think you can,
or you think you can't, you're right."
—Henry Ford

I believe mindset is the most overlooked and underrated factor in recovery. Our thoughts and our minds are so much more powerful than we give them credit for. Just like stress is an invisible factor that causes physiological responses in the body, our mindset does the same. Science has proven that our thoughts impact our bodies at a cellular level and can impact our lives and directly impact our health. During recovery, this is a hidden tool that we can harness and use to our advantage.

Dr. Mark Hyman, a *New York Times* best-selling author and leader in the world of functional medicine states that "mindset and what we believe is one of the most powerful tools we have when it comes to upleveling our health. Yet, many of us do not take advantage of this. We focus on what we eat, or how much we are exercising, but rarely do we focus on our thoughts." Think about the power of the placebo effect. What you think can affect physical outcomes.

Not only do most people not realize how powerful their minds are, most people would rather do just about anything other than sit in silence alone with their thoughts. In a study that gave people the option to either be alone in silence with their thoughts for fifteen minutes or receive an electric shock, thirty percent of women gave themselves the shock as did sixty percent of men. Not only is it boring, but thoughts can be nasty, brutal, and incessant. During recovery when we spend a lot of time in rest and in silence, we are forced to hang out with and endure our thoughts in a way that most people would never tolerate. Learning to not let them take hold of you, and more importantly, to choose ones that are intentional and productive can be a game changer.

During recovery, it often feels like we are trapped inside emotional chaos. Mindset work is about using tools to meet yourself underneath that chaos. From there, you can make choices more clearly, including choosing thoughts that will support your healing. You cannot choose all your thoughts; plenty of them arise automatically. But with practice, you can learn to spot them for what they are, just thoughts, not the truth, and let them pass by without gripping into you. On the flip side, you can also choose to think thoughts that will serve you well and promote healing from deep within, all the way down to the cellular level.

Mindset work is not about forced positivity, and it is not a replacement for mental health care. It is a tool you can use in addition to medical support. It's ultimately about creating habits and new neural pathways that will help move you forward in powerful ways. This takes practice, and we'll cover the tools that you need to use your mindset to help fuel your recovery throughout this chapter. I promise you, if you can learn to do this work now, it will serve you in big ways for the rest of your life.

Step 1: Know Your "Why"

Mindset work begins with you knowing your "why." Why are you committed to recovering? What or who are you doing it for? What is driving you forward? Getting clear on why you are committed to recovering is an important first step because it's easier to stay focused and motivated when you have a purpose. Depending on the severity of your injury and the duration of your recovery, you may need to dig deep here to come up with something very compelling.

I had a job and a life that I desperately wanted to get back to, but as I got increasingly worn down, that wasn't enough to pull me forward. I found that I needed something bigger to focus on that would give me the inspiration and motivation to keep doing the work.

What I desired most in my life at the time was to find purpose and fulfillment. I knew in my gut that there was a fire inside of me that wasn't getting used, and that I was meant to do something with a bigger impact than I was making through my job. This was something I had been thinking about a lot in the year leading up to my accident, and I used my recovery time to lean into the exploration. Dreaming up ways to share my story and make a difference in the recovery community when I was feeling better, no matter how long it took, became my passion, my purpose, and my fuel. You may want to improve your overall health so that you can accomplish a goal that feels out of reach right now, recover for your family, your partner, to get back to work, or to hike the Appalachian Trail. Whatever it is that pulls you forward, name it. It now becomes your "why" and your True North.

This was mine: "I am recovering so that I can become the healthiest, happiest, most peaceful and powerful version of myself."

Getting clear on your why, or your intention, keeps your conscious and subconscious mind hyper-oriented toward your goal. You will begin noticing opportunities and become open to ideas, inspiration, and actions that will move you in the direction of that outcome that you didn't see or weren't open to before. For me, getting clear on my big picture desire ultimately led to writing this book, launching a new career, and getting tapped into my passion and my purpose in a far greater way than I had imagined.

If you're at a loss for inspiration or feeling stuck, I recommend starting with journaling to help you get clear. You can free write or try starting with the journal prompt "I desire..." and see what comes up. Make a list of every desire you can think of. Take your time and keep peeling away the layers until you find something that really resonates with you.

Your job right now is not to know the *how*, it is only to identify the *what*.

Practice:

- Take time to sit and get clear on your why.

- If you are unsure, try using the journal prompt "I desire" and free write for a while to see what comes up.

- Review what you have written to identify what resonates most with you. Play around with it for a while until you have something that feels powerful and compelling.

Step 2: Use The Tools

Affirmations

Affirmations are brief phrases that help you get into both conscious and subconscious alignment with powerful, positive thoughts of your choosing. They are a tool for conditioning your mind and creating new neural pathways. I used them as a tool to get centered during long periods of silence when I was bored, restless, or in a bad place emotionally. I often paired my affirmations with slow deep breathing to help pass the time and reduce my anxiety. It helped bring me back to a place of peace.

Start by turning your intention or your why into an affirmation by switching it to the present tense, as if you have already accomplished it. For me this was:

"I am the healthiest, happiest, most peaceful and powerful version of myself. My recovery was so worth it".

You can also choose an affirmation centered around how you want to feel on a day-to-day basis, such as, "I am healthy and strong. My body is healing every day". Affirmations are personal and must resonate with you deeply. Explore and experiment until you find phrases that feel right to you.

Here are a few examples:

- My body is healthy and strong. I am healing every day.

- I am navigating recovery with peace and ease.

- I am healing at my own pace, and in my own time.

- I move my body every day with ease.

- I show up as the best version of myself for my family.

- I am strong enough to hike the Appalachian Trail.

After you've identified your affirmation, you've got to own it. Repeat it to yourself every morning and throughout the day whenever you think of it. I wrote mine out in Sharpie and taped it up on my wall where I would walk past it multiple times a day. I did my physical therapy exercises in front of it. When I needed a reminder, I would go and stare at it for a while. I repeated it to myself when I was lying down with my eye mask on. I repeated it so many times that it became ingrained into my subconscious. This commitment and repetition trains your mind to begin looking for opportunities to help make it happen.

Practice:

- Turn your recovery "why" into an affirmation by switching it into the present tense. For example, "I want to recover so that I can be present for my family" becomes "I am present for my family."

- Write out a number of thoughts or statements that help you feel strong and confident in your body's ability to heal and/or your resilience.

- Repeat them out loud or internally multiple times daily, especially any time you feel yourself spiraling into fear, worry, or negativity. Really own them.

Visualization

Visualization is a tried-and-true technique that can be used in multiple ways during recovery. Many of the world's top athletes, entrepreneurs, and peak performers use visualization as a performance enhancing tool. Why? Because visualization conditions the body toward a specific outcome. When we practice visualization, our body integrates the feeling of the experience or outcome we are picturing and orients our subconscious mind to make it happen. This is possible because our minds can't tell the difference between what we visualize and what has happened physically. Your body believes that what you are visualizing is actually happening, and with repetition, it creates deep internal muscle memory.

Take a minute to close your eyes and picture eating a lemon. Really picture yourself smelling it, tasting it, feeling the texture and the juice. Notice what is happening inside your mouth. Are you puckering? Are you salivating? Can you taste it? Your body is having a physical reaction to the visualization, not the physical experience of actually eating a lemon.

Visualization is a great tool for bringing your recovery intention to life. Visualize what it feels like to be healthy, strong, and pain-free. Visualize waking up with energy and clarity every day. Visualize being present with your family, your partner, or your friends. Visualize doing whatever it is you dream of doing on the other side of your recovery. This will help integrate those feelings into your body and train your subconscious mind to move in that direction without you even having to think about it.

It's also a great way to kill time when you're getting through a hard day, or to find a place of inner calm when you are struggling. Picture yourself in your happy place. Picture yourself on a beach. Try to let yourself go and truly sink into the peace of these settings.

I relied on visualization when there was a task I knew I needed to do, but felt stuck underneath my symptoms and was unable to get myself moving. At different times in my recovery, this was getting up to eat, getting pain medicine, going for a walk, or doing my physical therapy exercises.

With my eyes closed, I would picture myself getting up from bed or the couch and preparing a plate of food for myself, or getting up, putting my shoes on, and getting out for a walk. I would picture this over and over until my body shifted into action. I found that if I spent time visualizing, eventually, my body would find a tiny little break in my mood of otherwise not wanting to, and carry me up and in the direction of the task I had been focusing on. There were numerous times when I was stuck in bed but focused on where I was trying to go, and I would eventually find myself on my feet without having any awareness of having instructed myself to stand up. One minute I was stuck, the next minute, I was up. More than once, I found myself marveling, "Huh! Would you look at that!? This stuff actually works."

Start by taking a few deep breaths, close your eyes, and picture yourself doing whatever it is you need to do. Picture it so vividly that you feel like you are already in action. Here's the important part: Picture yourself doing whatever it is with *ease*. Imagine you are moving through the activity without resistance and completing it easily. Picture yourself engaged in the task until it feels real.

The resistance will slip away, and eventually, your body will carry you forward.

Practice:

- With your eyes closed, picture yourself on the other side of your recovery. Let the feeling of that strong, healthy future pull you forward today.

- Picture yourself feeling peaceful and pain free.

- With your eyes closed, picture yourself moving through today's tasks with ease.

Journal It Out

I'll confess that I generally resist journaling. Every time I actually sit down to write, however, it feels good. Sometimes it leaves me feeling focused and energized; other times, it leaves me feeling calmer if what I need to do is rant or rage about something. It works in all sorts of ways; you just have to sit down and do it. Several studies in recent years have indicated that journal writing improves immune function and increases levels of alertness, determination, and energy while lightening the mind and body through emotional release.[20] This is not something that needs to be done in a notebook with a unicorn on it; it is a practical tool that physically calms your body and clears stress.

For many months, my daily journal entries were diatribes about how crappy I was feeling, and it was cathartic to get it out on paper. Eventually, I started using journaling to help me focus on my recovery intention. Now I use it to focus on my big picture goals and what I am committed to accomplishing. You can use it in any way that feels good to you.

If it's too painful for your eyes to write in a physical notebook, use the voice memo app on your phone to dictate your daily entries. You can do this straight from bed—that's what I did for a long time.

Set aside a few minutes each morning to sit down and simply do a brain dump. Get out any thoughts or stresses weighing you down, or goals and intentions for the day. Or simply write how you are feeling. It's surprising the insights that show up when you sit down and write. Once they're out of your brain and onto the page, the stress and inner angst are reduced because you are no longer working so hard to contain them. You can also use journaling to bring your intentions and visualizations to life. The act of writing helps engrain them into your internal wiring even more.

Another great journaling tool to use is to write from your future self. Write from the "you" that is on the other side of recovery. How did you get there? What's it like? What do you know on the other side that you can't see from where you are now? Tell yourself what you learned along the way. Give yourself the guidance and assurance that you need to hear.

Here are a few journal prompts for getting started, depending on what sort of mood you're in:

- This is awful. Here's why ...

- Today I am committed to ...

- Today I desire to feel ...

- How am I going to make it through another day like this? I'll tell you how. I'm going to

- Write from your future self. What do you need to hear today? What would your future self like to tell you?

Practice:

- Sit down for a few minutes each morning to put your thoughts on paper and clear them from your head, or to get clear on what you will focus on for the day ahead.

- When you need guidance or support, write to yourself from a future version of you. The you that has made it through recovery and knows what you need to hear right now.

Gratitude

Science shows that there are ample positive benefits of a gratitude practice. Namely that it can rewire the brain and nervous system (for the better).[21] Traditional methods center on making a gratitude list first thing in the morning and the last thing before bed, but I often found that it hurt my eyes too much to write on paper, so I made this an internal activity that I turned to throughout the day when I needed to pull myself out from a pain or negativity spiral. I also found that making a mental gratitude list was a really good way to pass my brain-rest time in silence while guiding my mind away from stressful thoughts.

If you're in bed or on the couch, close your eyes and start thinking of and listing everything you are grateful for. Your bed. Your couch. Access to clean water. The food in your fridge, etc. Big or small, just riff on it for a while. Let this practice become a habit you integrate into your day more regularly. For example, I now end my day by running through a mental list of everything I'm grateful for from that day, from start to finish. It's how I unwind to go to sleep at night.

You could also keep a notebook beside your bed for the more traditional written approach— whatever works for you. By conditioning your mind to look for the positive, it will eventually begin looking for things to be grateful for all on its own. And when you pivot your mind to gratitude, it opens up an internal channel that's wired for peace, ease, and healing.

Practice:

- Take a few minutes to close your eyes and mentally list out everything you are grateful for.

- Keep a notebook beside your bed and write five to ten things you are grateful for, first thing after you wake up, and right before bed.

- If you catch yourself stuck in pain or an emotional spiral, make a gratitude list in that moment either in your mind or on paper to help break the cycle.

Meditation

Before my accident, I was a dabbler in meditation, and now I am a daily devotee. The benefits are incredible. Tuning in to meditation fills me with an overwhelming sense of peace, clarity, and energy that is addicting. Glennon Doyle shares in her beautiful book, *Untamed*, that she experiences a feeling of liquid gold running through her body during meditation.[22] Who doesn't want that?

Meditation was and still is one of my go-to tools for pain management. It can lower anxiety, lower your heart rate, clear away mental clutter, and literally make you happier (there is science behind this). Meditation also creates stillness in your mind so your intuition can be heard, which I think is important during recovery. Our intuition has all the answers. When I am stuck or overwhelmed, tuning in to meditation, even for just a few minutes, can bring me to a place of stillness where my intuition can pipe up with the guidance I need in that moment.

There is one hurdle here. Meditation is, by definition, exercise for the brain. When I first started meditating again after my injury, it actually made my head hurt worse. This both irritated and confused me. Isn't this supposed to make me feel better? More calm? What the hell!? I knew that the purported benefits of meditation were worthwhile, but I didn't want to cause myself more pain. So, I started and stopped, usually coming back to it when I was bored and I let my practice evolve over time.

Initially, I wasn't sure what I was doing or looking for. In the short term, it was a simple way to pass the time. Eventually, I came back to it more and more often, and with time, I could start feeling the benefits building. It hurt less, and to my surprise, I did feel calmer. Then it started feeling *good,* so I did it more consistently. In time, I got more comfortable with silence and really enjoyed the sense of inner stillness and expansion (and the occasional rush of liquid gold), and I turned to meditation or silence more than I turned to audiobooks or podcasts. I think this has been the biggest benefit of meditation for me. Learning to be content in silence and to give my mind space to truly relax and be calm. This trickles down to help your body relax and be calm.

On the pain management front, I was surprised to find that eventually, I was able to meditate myself out of pain. Not completely, and not every time, but enough that I keep going back for more. I am able to relax my mind and nervous system enough to let go of my mental attachment to the pain and somehow just float somewhere outside of it. It's still there, but it doesn't have the same effect on me. Meditation is powerful. It just takes practice and repetition.

Let's talk about the basics. There are three primary types of meditation, and you'll want to find one that feels good to you. I use all three in different situations. They are:

Breath work

Using your breath to focus your mind.

Visualization

Focusing your attention on a specific image or guided experience.

Mantra

Silently repeating a word or phrase to help you drop into a deeper meditative state.

Regardless of the method, the basic premise is this: Sit or lie comfortably somewhere quiet. (For a long while I meditated while lying on the couch. I now sit in a chair with my back supported by a pillow, feet flat on the ground, palms on my legs facing up.) Close your eyes and take a few slow, deep, centering breaths. Release any tension you are holding in your body. Your eyelids may flutter like crazy, which is a result of the injury. Let this be background noise; it doesn't matter. Now just let yourself be. Thoughts will run through your mind. Notice them and let them move on. Notice your thoughts, then return to the stillness in the center. Depending on the method you choose, you may also be using your breath, a visualization, or a mantra to focus on. That's it. Let your thoughts float by and keep coming back to center.

When you first start out, you'll likely be mired in thoughts and get pulled into things like, "This is so dumb. Why am I even doing this? Aren't I supposed to not be thinking right now? Aren't I supposed to be peaceful and still? This isn't working. Why do I suck at this?" Well, you are *not* supposed to not be thinking. Stopping your thoughts isn't possible. The practice is to notice your thoughts and let them pass, then come back to center. This is building a new muscle that will strengthen with repetition. Increasing slices of peace and stillness will come with time and practice. This will eventually spill over into your everyday life when you are not meditating. In recovery this is powerful because it balances the nervous system and creates space for healing to flow.

If you are curious about meditation but either get bored with it or feel like going it alone isn't working for you, I loved the book *Meditation for Fidgety Skeptics: A 10% Happier How-To Book* by ABC News Anchor Dan Harris and meditation teacher Jeff Warren.[23] It provides a wide range of simple guided meditations, some that I found particularly applicable to recovery. Harris wrote his first book, *10% Happier,* about his experience with meditation after living with PTSD and undergoing a panic attack on live television. He shares that meditation ultimately made him 10% happier, a concept I love. He does not promise the moon; he just shares how it can shift the needle a bit. That book is a great read, too. Harris's dry wit and general skepticism speak to me.

Here are a few practices for getting started with meditation:

Basic Meditation (I use this practice while lying in bed or on the couch on high-pain days)

Sit or lie comfortably.

Close your eyes and take a few slow, deep breaths.

Let your breathing neutralize, and keep your mind focused on the empty space between your thoughts.

As thoughts come and go, simply notice them and come back to center. Try not to get stuck in them. When you notice yourself stuck or down a rabbit hole, as soon as you notice it—that's it! You win! Gently move your mind back to center.

The entire practice is calm breathing and bringing your mind back to center.

Your mind will not be blank. If you are stuck in thoughts, stress, or anxiety and can't find "center," you are not doing it wrong. It's going to take some time to break through the noise. Once you find a small sliver of calm, trust that you will keep coming back to it, and it will continue expanding and unfolding over time.

Repeat for 5–10 minutes, more or less, depending on what feels good to you.

Note: It helps me to have a word or phrase (a mantra) to focus on. This helps you stay focused in the neutral space rather than going down thought tangents and will also help you drop into a deeper meditative state. Start by using simple words and phrases like, "may I be calm", or "may I be well", and just slowly repeat the phrase internally while you are breathing. This is not a forced or regimented repetition. Let it flow naturally. You can take this practice further by testing out additional guided mantra meditations through a meditation app.

Square Breathing

This breath work meditation is a great tool for calming the mind and engaging the vagus nerve to support balancing the nervous system. I like to use this at night if I can't sleep, and it can also be helpful to use for addressing anxiety and overwhelm. One woman shared with me that she uses this to help with her balance issues. It's quite simple:

Close your eyes.

Breathe in deeply and slowly for a count of four.

Hold your breath at the top for a count of four.

Exhale slowly for a count of four.

Hold at the bottom for a count of four.

Repeat until you are feeling calmer and more centered.

Note: You can do this for a count of six or eight if a longer, slower pace feels better to you. Breathing out for a longer count than you breathed in is another good practice for calming the nervous system. Do what feels good for you.

Healing Visualization

The goal of this meditation is to feel aligned with your body's inner healing energy. As you move through the visualization, imagine a column of pure white light that begins at the top of your head, radiates down along your spine, and exits out through your tailbone. Feel this energy getting dialed into alignment like a combination lock, ending up with one unobstructed pathway.

Lie comfortably, close your eyes, and take a few slow deep breaths, inhaling deeply and exhaling out any tension.

When you are ready, begin to visualize a soft white light entering through the top of your head, beginning to flow through your body down your spinal cord and out through your tailbone. With each breath, you are drawing in more and more of this pure healing light.

Breathing deeply, visualize this clean, bright, healing energy flowing, growing stronger and reaching further with each breath. Starting at the top of your head, down behind your eyes and through your throat, through your chest and down your abdomen, down to your tailbone and back out.

Picture your body being cleansed and healed by this beautiful light.

Continue breathing in this pure healing energy, pulling it through your entire body, healing your cells with each breath in and breathing out any toxins or blocks. Feel it running through you completely unobstructed for at least five cycles of breath.

When you are ready, release your focus, and slowly open your eyes.

Return to this visualization whenever you want to feel grounded, centered, or in alignment with your inner healing energy.

Guided Meditations

Many people benefit from guided meditations, especially when they are getting started. There are several great apps available with wide-ranging content. My favorite is the Chopra App created by Dr. Deepak Chopra—they have wonderful programs ranging from pain management to sleep and just about everything in between. It's focused on eastern traditions and uses Sanskrit mantras, so just be prepared for that vibe.

Additional apps include:

✓ Calm

✓ Headspace

✓ Insight Timer

✓ The Love Your Brain Foundation also offers free meditations on their website

Practice:

- Begin by taking a few minutes each day to sit in silence and practice one of the basic meditations mentioned above, or to explore a guided meditation from an app.

- Remember that different types of meditation work for different people. Take some time to explore what feels good to you.

- Meditation is a practice. It will get easier and feel better over time. Do not quit because you think it "isn't working." If you are showing up, it's working. Just keep showing up.

As we wrap up this chapter, start by choosing one or more of these tools and explore to see what feels good to you. Digging into this work and watching it affect my life in ways far beyond the healing process has been one of the greatest gifts of my recovery. I hope it will serve you in similar ways.

Now that we have covered the recovery essentials of hydration, sleep, movement, nutrition, and mindset, in the next section, we will get into more nitty-gritty tools for getting through the days.

KEY TAKEAWAYS

✓ Identify your recovery "why." Make it powerful.

✓ Create affirmations to bring your goals and desires to life.

✓ Practice visualization to engrain feelings of progress and lightness into your body.

✓ Use journaling to release your emotions or tap into your inner guidance.

✓ Use a gratitude practice to help pull yourself out from a negativity spiral.

✓ Explore different styles of meditation to find one that resonates with you. Start small, stick with it, and trust that your practice will expand over time.

PART THREE

Getting Through the Days

Chapter 7

Getting Through the Days

"We can do hard things."
–Glennon Doyle

As you know by now, the first pillar of recovery is having a strategic treatment program in place. The second is to make sure you're doing everything you can to support your body's recovery with hydration, nutrition, sleep, movement, and mindset. But what happens after that? Those things are foundations; they are not ways to actually get through the days.

When I got to the point that it was months between doctor's appointments and I was still in severe pain without much hope for improvement, I got desperate and depressed. I felt lost and alone for the day-to-day. It's one thing to know that recovery takes time, and that progress is not linear, and quite another to live with the pain and uncertainty day in and day out. One of the questions I asked most frequently was, "How do people *do* this? How do they get through the days?" I even asked this question to my doctor. He did not have an answer.

Sometimes, even for long stretches of time, I felt absolutely stuck. Stuck in pain, stuck in bed, stuck with my eye mask on, in fear about finances, feeling like I wasn't making progress, not knowing how to ask for help, and the list goes on. I was bored, confused, and afraid all at the same time and it was a ruthless cycle. So much of getting through a day was learning how to get myself unstuck and to move forward, or unstuck mentally and at peace with resting, or accepting that sometimes not making progress is still progress. Sometimes just getting through the day *is* progress. Learning to coach myself through the days (and many sleepless nights) took a long time and a lot of practice. It required frequent calls to friends and family for support, but eventually I gathered up some tools and strategies that worked well for me. I share those tools in detail in this chapter.

If you're looking for the short answer to "How do you get through it?" the most basic truth is, you just do. You just keep going. You keep hold of belief in yourself and your body and keep putting one foot in front of the other (or allow yourself to rest until you've got enough energy to move the next foot). The question to ask yourself is, are your feet pointed in the right direction? If they are, use the tools in this chapter to keep yourself moving forward. If something is off, use the information from the previous chapters to make adjustments and *then* keep moving forward. Tiny little steps add up in the long run and will get you where you're trying to go.

Ultimately, each of us needs to find ways to get through the days that work for us. Here are the things that helped me the most.

Managing the Days

Use a Spiral Notebook

The most helpful thing I did to function with my cognitive symptoms and memory impairment was to write everything down in a spiral notebook that I kept open on the kitchen counter. This was different from my journal. It was essentially a running list of everything that came up throughout the day that I needed to remember. For example, I wrote down if I took my morning pills and when I took my pain medicine. I wrote out my (small) daily to-do list. I took notes on my symptoms and wrote down the questions I wanted to ask my providers the next time I saw them. I also took notes on the things that were stressing me out that I needed to ask for help with. It was my central command station.

I found that keeping the notebook open to that day's page at all times was important so I could easily write things down when passing by. If it was sitting there closed, I would just walk straight past it.

This system was not perfect. I remember one day, I took my pain medicine and set the bottle back down on the counter. Before writing down that I had taken it, I turned away for a moment. When I came back to the notebook a few seconds later, I couldn't remember whether or not I had taken the pill, and I got so frustrated and overwhelmed that I started crying. But things like this got better with time.

Utilize Voice Prompts

I do not consider myself to be technologically savvy, so it took some time for me to learn this one, but when I did it was a game-changer. Siri will read your text messages to you if you ask her to. Just say, "Hey Siri, read me my messages." She will also write responses. You can also say, "Hey Siri, write a new note that says…" if you want to file a note or to-do items for later. I used this often to clear things out of my head when I didn't have any paper handy. For Android users, this can be done by installing the Voice Access app.

For a long time, I used voice memos for keeping track of questions for my doctors. I would create a new one every time a question popped into my head. Then, before my next appointment, I would review them and transfer them to my spiral notebook.

I also use an Amazon Echo Dot to remind me to get ready for my appointments, which makes a big difference for me. I find that always keeping one eye on the clock in order to leave on time for things is a major mental battery drain. I just say, "Alexa, remind me at 2:30 p.m. to get ready for PT," etc. I also use Alexa to set timers when I'm doing activities that I know need to be time limited to keep my symptoms in check.

Pacing

One of the most useful tips I learned from a physical therapist about pacing my days was the "red light, yellow light, green light" scale for monitoring symptoms.

It works like this: On a scale of 1–10, assign yourself a baseline number for your average pain level. This is your starting point. From there, you are considered in "green light" until your symptoms have risen 3 or more points. When you're in green light it's business as usual, and you can continue with your activities.

Once your symptoms have increased 3 or more points, you're in yellow light. It's time to rest until your symptoms come back down to green. You've hit red light once your symptoms have increased 6 or more points. This means you did too much too soon. I call red light "falling through the ice". For me, once I got there, it could be days or weeks before things calmed down again. I really did not want to fall through the ice.

When you're in yellow or red light, turn to symptom and pain management tools like breath work, visualization, or meditation to help settle your nervous system. Rest or slow down until you are back in green light. For years, once I was in yellow light, I rarely came back down to green on the same day. I knew that I was resting until further notice, which was a very good motivator to monitor my status closely and try to stay in the green. That said, most days, I couldn't keep myself in green no matter how hard I tried. The threshold was so low and the triggers so difficult to avoid that it was nearly impossible to keep things in check. But this progressed and improved over time.

Here are a few tips for keeping yourself from veering into yellow and red:

✓ Move through tasks slowly.

✓ Check in with your body often.

✓ Set timers and take breaks.

✓ Learn the warning signs and how to notice when your symptoms are increasing, notch by notch.

✓ Your tolerance will gradually increase over time, but only if you don't regularly blow past your limits. Remind yourself that going slow is the work right now. When I first started writing this book, I could handle 25 minutes of screen time or cognitive work before I needed a break of at least 30 minutes, and I could do no more than an hour cumulatively per day. By the time I was finished with the book a year and a half later, I could handle increments of an hour and a half and a total of five hours per day. Even though progress was slow, the graduated progression worked.

If you are consistently on the upper end of the pain scale or landing in red light all the time, check in with your care team. You may not be ready to use this strategy yet and there are likely underlying issues that need to be addressed and worked through first.

Create Clear Reminders

At some point in my recovery, I started making signs for myself and taping them up in the primary hallway of my home. They were a combination of motivational quotes and mantras, and messages to myself that I needed to be reminded of frequently. Walking by them multiple times every day helped me internalize them.

"Go slow, check in, listen" is one of the first signs I put up. I needed the reminder to stop and check in with my body often because I tended to overdo it with activities and dig myself into deep holes. Each time I saw or remembered the sign, I would stop and check in with myself. Frequently this would trigger the realization that I needed to slow down and take a break or simply give myself permission to rest.

Over time, I built up an entire wall of these signs that looked a little bit like an FBI investigation board. Sometimes I would go stand in front of it to scan the list and look for whatever I needed to hear in that moment, and it helped!

Single-Tasking

Multi-tasking is a no-go during recovery. It's too much for the brain to handle. Now is the time for single-tasking. For me, this includes no music or podcasts while I am walking, no music while I am driving, and not trying to hold multiple thoughts or tasks in my head at once. One thing at a time. No background noise.

Pay Attention to Your Battery Drains

Overstimulation is a real thing. Music may drain your energy, or maybe it's heat, light, talking to people, or visual stimulation. Be aware of all these things and how they impact your energy and symptoms so that you can mitigate or plan accordingly. You may not be able to avoid some things, but you can plan to know that you will need to rest before and after certain situations.

Additionally, if you find that an activity or household chore zaps your energy, pay attention. This is important information. It may be something that you need to eliminate from your day, outsource, ask for help with, or use a timer to monitor your time spent on this activity. Remember that you need to preserve enough energy to go toward recovery to heal and to keep yourself from falling through the ice.

One Step at a Time

Figure out what you need to do next and take the next step—one step at a time. Often these steps are tiny and don't feel like they count, but tiny steps add up. For example, maybe the next thing is for you to take a walk. If getting out the door seems too hard, break it up into steps. The next step may be sitting up; then it's getting out of bed. Then it's finding your shoes, etc... You may even need to rest between steps, and that's ok.

Sometimes the next thing to do *is* rest.

Release Your Emotions

The crying. Oh, the crying! The anxiety, anger, depression, irritability, and overwhelm. Acknowledge these feelings when they arise and allow them to release. Let them flow so they will pass. Keeping emotions bottled up when they flare increases stress, pain, and anxiety. Make sure you are plugged into a supportive community (we will cover this more in Chapter 10) and that you are working with a mental health professional who can support you with techniques for safe and effective emotional processing and release. This stuff needs to come out and, if stored internally, may be a block to recovery.

Let New Routines Unfold

I am a person who likes structure and routine. Not following one has been one of the most difficult adjustments I have made during recovery. To be honest, I still struggle with this but I find that because my symptoms don't keep to a schedule, it's nearly impossible for me to stick to one either.

Over time, I have realized that if I simply let the day unfold in its own time and follow whatever my energy cycle is that day, if I am clear on my priorities, the most important things get done. This is not the same as doing everything I want to do in a day. This means the really, truly important things get done and the others fall away. Trust that your capacity and consistency will increase over time.

Utilize Free Audio Content

At this point, you may be wondering, "Okay, but what did you actually *do* all day?" I primarily relied on audiobooks and podcasts to fill my time (although these things are not brain rest, and I still spent a lot of time in silence). I alternated between two apps offering free audiobook downloads with a public library membership: Libby and Hoopla. Podcasts are another great free resource.

I found that different types of content were different levels of taxing for my brain. For example, podcasts were more taxing than novels. I would keep a few options at the ready and alternate based on what I was in the mood for or could tolerate on any given day.

If you struggle with screen time, ask a friend or family member to search for and download a few books and podcasts for you and keep you loaded up so you don't need to scroll through your phone searching for something new when it's time.

Self-Care

You are doing a hard thing right now. This hard thing requires energy, discipline, stamina, courage, and resilience. When was the last time you did something nice for yourself? I know it can seem hard to find things that feel good during recovery, but it's so important to feed your soul when you are asking so much of your body for healing day in and day out.

Self-care and treats for yourself don't need to be expensive. What feels good to you will differ based on life and recovery circumstances, but I encourage you to prioritize this. Prioritize yourself, the one who is doing the hard work.

My favorite "treat" was to lie on the couch or in bed with a cozy blanket and listen to a feel-good audiobook. Over the first winter, I took weekly bubble baths or magnesium soaks, or took a clearing bath (one pound of Epsom salts and one pound of baking soda in warm water, not hot) to help relax myself and my body. Clearing baths are particularly amazing for releasing stress. Sometimes I did something as simple as massaging my hands and feet with lotion, or resting with a warm pack on my chest or neck while doing some deep breathing or meditation.

Self-care may also mean taking a break from your recovery program. Maybe you need a week off from appointments to rest, or you skip your PT exercises for a few days. It's ok to take breaks to refill your tank.

These gentle touches can help renew your spirit and energy to help you keep going.

Speak to Yourself as You Would to a Friend

Finally, if you catch yourself in a negativity spiral or being hard on yourself, ask yourself what you would say to a friend if they were in your shoes. Usually, my internal dialogue was harsh and demanding in a way that I would never speak to somebody who I cared about and had compassion for. Go ahead and give yourself the same feedback, wisdom, insight, or pep talk you would give to someone you love.

Remember, your body and your brain are functioning very differently right now than they used do. This is about finding creative solutions that work for you and supporting your individual recovery priorities and needs. Allow your body to guide you and do what feels right for you each day.

On the extra hard days, these tools may not be enough. In the next chapter, I'll be going over some techniques to try when you're feeling stuck.

KEY TAKEAWAYS

✓ Using specific strategies to guide yourself through each day can help you stay on track and moving forward. This often requires stepping outside of yourself and thinking about how you can best support yourself in any given moment.

✓ Be intentional about finding tools and techniques that feel good to you.

✓ Identify a simple self-care practice you can turn to daily or weekly.

✓ When you need help getting on track, consider what you would say to a friend who was in your shoes.

Chapter 8

Techniques to Try
When You're Feeling Stuck

"Almost anything will work again if you unplug it for a few minutes, including you." –Anne Lamott

It is so easy to get stuck when you are in pain, especially chronic pain. It wears you down. I found myself "stuck" on the couch or in bed countless times, unable to get up to get food, pain medicine, go for a walk, etc. Or stuck mentally, unsure how to continue moving through a hard day. Some days the pain was stronger than I was, and that's just how it went. Over time, I learned a few methods for getting myself unstuck. In this chapter I'll share what worked for me.

Ask Yourself: What Would Be Good for Me Right Now?

I know this seems simple, but actually taking the step back to get clear is powerful. The answer might be Tylenol, a snack, a walk, a nap, or reaching out to someone for support. Whatever comes up is the next thing to focus on.

Establishing what might help me feel better, whether physically or emotionally, and setting my sights on moving toward taking action was usually satisfying—even if also challenging. Overcoming the challenge was even more satisfying. Taking control of the situation, establishing what my body needed, and taking action helped me feel like I wasn't going down with the ship.

Visualization

Set your sights on where you're trying to go (e.g., getting up to get a snack). Picture yourself doing the task until it feels real. When you have a clear vision, things start to align themselves accordingly. Stay open and trust that your body will take you where you want to go if you let it. The key here is to stay open. I found that if I let my mind wander rather than stay focused on and locked into the pain, my body would get me up and going without me even thinking about it.

Use the "Let's Just See" Method

Say to yourself, "Let's just see what happens if I go for a walk right now," or "Let's just see what happens if I get up to get a glass of water..." and give it a shot. This one requires a little more than letting your body carry you on its own, but it's a good technique to help you get started.

Clear the Path

Identify what is in the way for you right now. What is blocking your progress or causing you anxiety? Often when we are stuck, it's because we aren't acknowledging what's really going on. Are you stressed because your calendar is too full? Perhaps you need groceries and aren't capable of getting out to the store. Do you not have the proper emotional support? Is it because your life demands you to push too hard? Acknowledging what is in the way is the first step and may even result in a feeling of relief. Then when you are ready, you can take the next step toward addressing the obstacle and clearing the path.

Move Your Body

An object in motion stays in motion, and an object at rest stays at rest. Start by getting up from wherever you are resting and move around the house. This may be enough of an energy boost to get you out for a walk if that's your goal, or to start getting dinner ready, etc. This is good for when you have a little energy and need to move in the direction of whatever task is next for you, but the "big task" feels too daunting. Just start.

Close Some Tabs in Your Brain

Think of your brain as a computer. When you have too many tabs open, it gets bogged down and starts running slow. Figure out what tabs you can close to create some more mental space. This may mean making your plan for dinner so you're no longer worried about it, canceling that thing on your calendar, or calling a friend or family member to come over for support to help you manage what's on your plate.

Make a Mental Gratitude List

Even though we've covered this before, I want to drop it in again here. The distraction of this exercise helps pull you out of whatever you are stuck in and frees you up for your body and mind to make a move in the direction you want to go.

Take Baby Steps

Often, taking the first step is the hardest part. Just get started. When going for a walk is too daunting, start by putting on your shoes. Maybe just getting your shoes on is the win for that day. Tomorrow you can put on your shoes *and* your coat, etcetera...When getting out of bed feels too hard, start by just sitting up. Progress breeds progress. Small steps add up. Little victories build momentum.

When in Doubt, Zoom Out

When you are overwhelmed or don't know what to do next, perspective always helps. Zoom out. Drink a glass of water. Take a walk or get outside if you are able, or close your eyes and take a few deep breaths. Remind yourself of your "why." Perspective creates space for you to realign with your intentions and take the next right step.

Guardrails

If all the above failed to help and I couldn't get myself centered or grounded, I used the following reminders to get myself back on track (or at least to slow the downward spiral). These were taped up on my wall, too. When necessary, I would review this list to identify where I was getting stuck. Once I found it, it was like identifying that I had bumped up against a guardrail and needed to make a simple adjustment to get back on course.

What You Focus On Grows

If you focus on your progress, you will see more progress. If you focus on your desire to be more physically active, you will become more physically active. Or if you focus on your desire for improved sleep, you will begin to make more changes to improve your sleep. Be very intentional about what you focus on and think about, because these are things you will see and experience more of.

Ask yourself: Do I need to shift what I am focusing on?

What You Resist Persists

On the flip side, if you focus on how mad you are that you still have a headache, your headache will increase. If you focus on how frustrated you are that it's so difficult to navigate the medical system, that frustration will persist. If you catch yourself in a cycle of negativity, make a pivot. Focus on something you desire more of.

Ask yourself: Am I fighting against or resisting something right now? What is it? How can I let this go or refocus my thoughts? What does this look like from a wider perspective?

The Magic Is in the Margins

Recovery requires time and space. The more margin you create in your life (by margin I mean blank space), the more healing can occur, and the more your intuition can speak up with guidance and direction for what you need next. This may mean clearing your calendar for the next few days or weeks, saying "no" to some things, or simply spending time in silence rather than listening to an audiobook. Progress and guidance show up when they have the space to.

Ask yourself: Do I need to create more margin right now? If so, how can I make that happen?

The Things That Got Easier Over Time

If you are feeling overwhelmed by the uncertainty of your recovery, or are discouraged that your symptoms are dragging on, trust that there are things that will get easier over time. Here's what improved for me along the way.

Letting the Emotional Storms Pass

I experienced severe emotional symptoms after my injury, particularly anxiety and overwhelm that manifested into extreme panic attacks, sometimes to the point of hyperventilation. It took a long time (over a year), plus therapy and medication, but I eventually learned how not to get stuck in the emotional storms when they hit. Instead, I learned to ride them out and let them pass. It is possible to choose not to "hook" into negative emotions, but instead let them run their course. Harvard trained neuroscientist Dr. Jill Bolte Taylor goes into the science of how this works in her fabulous book, *My Stroke of Insight*, about her experience recovering from a massive stroke in her thirties. I discovered it to be true firsthand.[24]

Rather than get stuck in emotional quicksand when the symptoms flared, I was eventually able to recognize the symptoms for what they were, symptoms. I knew they weren't permanent and that if I let them, they would pass. Sometimes I would picture myself sitting inside a raging storm and practice deep breathing and stillness while I waited for the storm to move on. Eventually, it would. This is not to say that it became easy to withstand, but the perspective helped. I let the tears flow, the anger rage, or the physical symptoms of a panic attack run their course while focusing on supporting myself through to the other side. Working with a therapist and having emotional support from friends and family while I worked through this was crucial.

Noticing the Yellow Lights and Stop Signs

About a year and a half into my recovery, my pain calmed down enough that if I didn't overdo it with activity, I could keep my symptoms at a more manageable level. There was still significant pain and dysfunction, but not enough to drive me to tears on a regular basis. I eventually learned to notice the early signs of nearing my activity limit, or the blaring warnings when I was overdoing it. Having even the smallest amount of control over keeping myself from falling through the ice was a huge accomplishment, and paved the way for more progress.

Prioritizing Recovery

This one was really hard. It took me a full year before I understood that if I didn't put recovery first, it was not going to happen. Then another seven months before the breaking point that got me to finally step away from work.

Prioritizing recovery also meant simpler things, like acknolwledging that I needed a lot of sleep and an open calendar at nearly all times (other than medical and other essential appointments) and accepting that many communications and life tasks would have to go unanswered and untended to. It took a lot of work to accept these things and preserve my energy for recovery and appointments, but I got there eventually. I could feel the difference in my body and the speed of my improvement when I did.

Whenever you find yourself stuck, remind yourself that it's okay, and that it's part of the process. Also remind yourself that it will get easier with time. My hope for you is that each day, even if you are feeling stuck, you trust in your body's ability to heal, listen to and trust your intuition, and keep taking the next step, one step at a time.

Now that we have covered the internal work of getting through the days, we will discuss outside support and external resources in the next chapter.

KEY TAKEAWAYS

✓ It is very easy to get stuck when you are dealing with concussion symptoms. This is normal.

✓ Once you are aware that you are stuck, you can choose tools to gently guide yourself forward.

✓ Use tools like the "let's just see" method or "just start" to get your body moving and in action. Remember that what you focus on grows, what you resist persists, and that the magic is in the margins.

✓ Work with a therapist for support and bring your friends and family into the reality of your situation so that they can support you too.

✓ Trust that over time it will all get easier.

CHAPTER 9

Support

"The power of community to create health is far greater than any physician, clinic, or hospital." –Dr. Mark Hyman

It is well documented that people with strong social support during health challenges have better recovery outcomes. We are social creatures who need social support, but asking for help is difficult for most of us. If this is you, now is an important time to break through that barrier. By bringing in outside help, love, emotional and logistical support, you free up energy and create more space for yourself to heal. It's also helpful to find a positive community of people who understand what you are going through.

During my recovery, I found that I needed a lot of help, but I didn't have the executive functioning skills to think through what people could actually help me with or the capacity to communicate or coordinate much.

I navigated this by keeping the circle of people I communicated with small. The people on the inside knew exactly what was going on and knew how to update and engage others who wanted to help, that I did not have the capacity to engage with. This helped me protect my energy and kept me from having to explain the situation, or update people every time we talked, which was emotional and draining for me.

Below is a list of the most helpful things my friends and family did to support me. If you are struggling with how to ask for help, let this list be a guide with suggestions on what to ask for. You could even just hand this book to a friend or family member, ask them to read this chapter and go from there.

If it feels difficult for you to accept help, remind yourself that people *want* to help. We are wired to want to support each other; so, plug your people in where you need them and let them. It will be a gift to you both.

Making To-Do Lists and Delegating Tasks

Multiple friends helped me with this, and oh man, was it helpful. I was so overwhelmed by all the things that needed to happen to keep my life moving:

- communicating with doctors
- scheduling appointments
- refilling prescriptions
- routine housekeeping
- emptying the dishwasher
- doing laundry

- keeping myself fed

- Answering e-mails

- etc.

These are basic things that normally would have been easy, but with a concussion felt nearly impossible.

A friend would ask me which things were floating around in my head and stressing me out, and we made a to-do list together (my friend would actually make the list; it was too overwhelming for me to do this on my own). Then we would work through it together to figure out which things could be outsourced. And here's what's important—she would actually do the outsourcing for me. The work of making the list, thinking through who could help, making contact, and giving instructions were all too much for me to handle. So, taking this load off my plate was hugely helpful—not just because it cleared the decks, but also because it decreased my stress and symptoms.

Research

If you are feeling lost or confused about what to do or where to go next, ask a friend or loved one to research the specialists and treatments available for your symptoms and in your area. Again, you can hand them this book. Then have them make any necessary phone calls to find out if providers are a good fit for you before scheduling.

Managing Communications

I found it overwhelming to receive calls and text messages because I was rarely able to respond, and I felt guilty for not keeping up with communications. Having friends and family members willing to send updates to people or respond to texts, calls, and emails took a lot of stress off my plate. I often felt bogged down by leaving communications unanswered, especially the longer my recovery dragged on.

Ask someone to get a rundown on who has reached out over the last week (or however long) or what personal business items need to be taken care of and do the work of responding, either directly from your phone or account, or from their own. Have them make it clear in the response that you aren't able to text right now, but you wanted to thank them for reaching out.

It's also helpful to have someone proactively manage communications and send updates to friends and family so there isn't a need to go through updates with each person each time they reach out.

As we were reviewing this chapter together, a friend also suggested that it would have been helpful if I had made a broad announcement or set up an automatic reply to e-mails and text messages, notifying people that I was dealing with a health issue and would take longer than normal to respond. I resisted this because I was trying to proceed as normal and didn't want people to know that I was struggling; but in hindsight, this would have alleviated a lot of pressure on me.

I also want to remind you that it's okay to let things go unanswered and to not have guilt about it. You will get back to people when you can, or you won't, and they will understand, or they won't. Either way is okay. The priority right now is you.

Errands

Ask someone to block out a chunk of time and run whatever errands need running, or ask them to text you when they are out running their own errands and see what they can accomplish for you while they are out. Some of the best texts I got said, "I'm at Target. What can I bring you?" Or "I'm going to Trader Joe's tomorrow. Give me your list!"

Help with Groceries and Meal Prep

Making sure the house is stocked with good healthy food that supports recovery can be a tall order when you can't handle going to the store. I had one friend in particular who would help me make my list and then pick up my groceries when she was out getting hers. Sometimes she would come to my house, and sometimes we would do it by phone. I also gave my friends access to my online grocery account so they could log in and order via a delivery service on my behalf when I couldn't handle the screen time.

I am lucky to have friends who love to cook and are familiar with meal prep, and they would often offer to go grocery shopping and then get me set up for the week. I would rest while they chopped vegetables, made egg cups, or prepped dinner(s) or freezer meals. They would also take care of cleaning, taking out the garbage, and other miscellaneous household tasks while they were over, which made a huge difference to my overall well-being and stress level.

Meal Delivery Service

My boss signed me up for a meal delivery service as a gift, and it was incredible. We used Sunbasket, which sends fresh, high-quality ingredients and simple recipes that you prepare on your own. Sometimes the cooking was still too much for me to handle, but having the food in the house for someone else to prepare if needed made a big difference. There are lots of different options for delivery services, including ones that do all the prep work for you or send fully prepared meals that you just reheat. A few good options are Sunbasket, HelloFresh, and Blue Apron. Local options may also be available in your community.

Driving

It was not safe for me to drive for a very long time. I also got nauseous in cars and needed to wear my eye mask on longer trips. I lived in a large city, so Uber, Lyft, and taxis were readily available, but I was so sensitive to smells that I avoided getting into a stranger's car that may have an air freshener in it at all costs. I also relied on public transit, but that flared my symptoms significantly so I tried to have friends drive me when I could.

Moral Support

I had a roster of friends and family available for serious moral support. They were on board to receive phone calls when I was overwhelmed, depressed or anxious, sometimes to the point of sobbing and unable to talk much. I would put the phone on speaker and set it down while I cried so I would feel less alone. Knowing there were people who were up to speed on the situation that I could call when I needed was priceless. The key here was that they were on the inside of what was happening and did not require me to give any sort of update. I could just call and say, "I need to cry right now," or "I'm having a panic attack," and then let it out.

Pre-Load Audio Content

Audio content was often my go-to for getting through the days. However, I couldn't handle the screen time to get these things downloaded onto my phone. Ask a friend to pre-load a bunch of podcasts or audiobooks for you, and make sure the app is on the first screen of your phone or tablet for easy access.

Try to find things that are gentle to listen to and not cognitively strenuous. For me this was novels.

Support with Medical Appointments

It's a big burden lifted to have someone help schedule appointments, accompany you to take notes and ask questions, and assist with follow-up items as needed.

I often had my mom accompany me to my appointments, and she was able to fill in more information for the doctor than I could recall myself. This was very important for making sure the doctor was getting the full picture from someone who had a broader perspective and more insight than I did. It was also important to have another person who was able to communicate with my medical team on my behalf if I was unable to do so on my own.

Online Support Resources

In addition to hands-on support from those around you for life tasks, there are wonderful online support communities where you can connect with others who are going through a similar experience. As I mentioned earlier, there are a few paid support communities as well as many free groups and programs. The options are expanding rapidly right now, so I recommend looking around to find a group that appeals to you. If this is too overwhelming, ask a friend or family member to investigate this for you. As a bonus, they will likely discover that there are also support groups available for loved ones and caregivers too.

Free Support Programs

- The Brain Injury Association of America has individual state-based associations that offer specialized local resources and support groups.

- The Love Your Brain Foundation offers a free 6-week online mindset program that includes go-at-your-own-pace resources and online meetups with group discussion. They also offer special groups for veterans, athletes, young adults, older adults, members of racially and/or ethnically non-dominant groups, and the LGBTQIA+ community.

Instagram

Instagram has a treasure trove of resources and beautiful souls sharing their recovery stories. Accounts evolve, start and end, so be sure to do a search to find people whose stories and content resonate with you. Start by typing "concussion" in the search bar to see what accounts come up, or by searching hashtags like #concussionrecovery, #concussionsupport, and #concussioneducation. Here are a few accounts I love to follow:

- Alison.rheaume
- Braininjuryhope
- Concussionrescue
- Theconcussioncommunity
- Thespooniementor
- Postconcussioninc
- Theconcussedslp

Many of these folks also host podcasts and free support groups. This list is just the beginning. I know there are many other wonderful accounts out there. Look around to find ones that resonates with you.

In addition to outside support, the support you give yourself is equally important. The next chapter covers how I kept track of all the things I needed to remember to keep myself moving forward.

KEY TAKEAWAYS

✓ People experiencing medical challenges are documented as having better outcomes if they have strong social support. Now is the time to ask for help from those around you.

✓ If that is too overwhelming, ask someone to do the outreach and coordination for you.

✓ If you aren't sure how to start, begin by handing this book over to a friend or loved one to read this chapter.

✓ If you don't have a supportive community around you and you want to get plugged in with people who understand what you are going through, look to online resources for help.

✓ Ask a friend or family member to help you research and navigate online support resources and support groups if you need help.

Chapter 10

Post-Its

"On the other side of a storm is the strength that comes from having navigated through it. Raise your sail and begin."
—Gregory S. Williams

H aving a toolbox full of tools is one thing. Finding what you need when you need it is quite another. In this chapter, we'll talk about how to be your own guide. After all, you are the one who knows what you need to hear or be reminded of at any given moment. For this, post-its were my best friend.

Over time, I started adding post-its to my motivational wall and moved them around the house as needed. It was a big freaking mess, but it contained everything I needed to hear, all in one place in a way that didn't require me to Rolodex through my brain to remember anything. When I would spiral or get stuck, I'd walk over to the wall and scan the signs and reminders to find what I needed to hear at that time. Having them up on the wall helped because even if I didn't stop to look at them, the messages would just seep in when I walked past.

Here are the ones that helped me the most:

What do you need right now?

This is such a simple but centering reminder. Each time I saw this note, I would stop, take a beat, and ask myself what I needed right then. Often, the answer would pop up before I even had the question out.

Sometimes what came up as the next thing to do didn't make sense, and I learned that is okay. Many times for me, it was "Go get a drink of water," which seemed ridiculous, but once I got to the kitchen, I realized what I really needed was to rest on the adjacent couch for a while. The next thing I actually needed was to move toward the couch, and getting a drink of water was a stepping stone to get me there.

We don't always get to know the full plan right up front, but we do always get an answer once we've learned how to hear it. Our bodies and intuition are smart and will guide us in the right direction if we listen. This is a muscle that you'll strengthen over time. It will become easier to hear the answers once you've been practicing for a while. Our job is to listen and trust. Ask yourself: *What is the next thing I need in order to progress?* Check in with yourself right now and ask. Then listen and trust. Another good question to ask is: *What do I need to hear right now?*

Closed for business.

This one was tactical, and I moved it around the house as needed. I would slap it on top of my phone, or my laptop, or my office door, or the TV as a reminder that I was not doing those things right now. It would make me stop and think before proceeding.

It's always darkest before the dawn.

This is kitschy, yes, but also practical and true. I noticed a frequent pattern that after I entered a stretch of extreme symptom flare-ups, I would often come out on the other side of it with my baseline one notch higher. Usually, my headaches or energy had improved a little bit. But despite this awareness, whenever I did enter a period of increased symptoms, my anxiety and fear would spiral. "What if this never gets better!? How am I going to keep living like this!?" The only tool I could offer myself at times like this was the reminder that it may just be a period of growing pains, and that I would emerge in a better place in a few days. Progress is often on the other side of discomfort.

What would you say to a friend right now?

We've covered this one before, but if your internal dialogue sounds anything like mine did, I think it's worth repeating. Most of my internal self-talk during my recovery was pretty nasty. It sounded like:

Why aren't you working harder?
Why are you making such a big deal about this?
Why don't you just suck it up and move on?
You are so lazy; you should be doing something right now,
etc.

This was not helpful, and is in fact harmful. I needed the reminder to reframe.

Let progress unfold.

Recovery happens in its own time, and there is no way to get a visual of where you are in the process. Trust that it is unfolding. Sometimes the discipline is in letting things progress in their own time and in their own way. I promise that when you stop holding on so tight, small wins (and big wins) will begin presenting themselves.

Be open to creative solutions.

Over time, I learned that if I let go of how things "should" go, I could find new ways to make things work. For example, my family gets together for dinner on Sundays. I could not handle the stimulation of being in a room with everybody, especially my young nieces and nephew. Listening to a conversation at the table was too painful, and I could not handle the sound of background music, or more than one voice talking at once. After a few awkward dinners where they had to turn off the music, and basically nobody talked, rather than stay home, I realized I could just eat in a different room than everybody else. I often rested in a different room, too, while everybody was hanging out pre or post-dinner. It wasn't perfect, and it still flared me up some, but I got the feel-good benefit of being able to somewhat participate with the family and not feel left out.

Celebrate your progress.

Got out of bed today? Celebrate. Went for a walk today, even for 5 minutes? Celebrate. Did your PT exercises today? Celebrate. Didn't cry today? Celebrate. You and your body are doing hard work. Honor it. This not only gives you a small hit of dopamine, the happiness hormone, but it also creates momentum.

Awesome wins.

If at this point, you are having any doubts about your recovery, or yourself, or how you're handling it, there are a few things I want to say to you. If you are sailing along smoothly, feel free to skip this part. But for the rest of you, it's important to me to put this on paper, mostly because it's what I needed to hear myself.

> *Listen.*
> *This. Shit. Is. Hard.*
> *You are not making it up.*
> *Unless you are pushing yourself too hard, you are not doing it wrong.*
> *Take this one step at a time.*
> *Meet yourself where you are.*

Ask for help.

If you don't know what to ask for, tell somebody that you need help but don't know what to ask for. Hand them this book to read.

Pay attention to your symptoms. Listen to what they are telling you. Take action accordingly. The next action may be to wait or to rest.

While you are waiting, believe in your body.

Believe that you are making progress every day. Say it, visualize it, write it, read it, repeat it. This matters.

This is hard, but you can do it. You are doing it, and you are awesome.

Just. Keep. Going.

Awesome wins.

I hope this is a chapter you will dog-ear and come back to any time you need to hear these things, or that you will start writing your own notes with your own messages to yourself. It may be a little eccentric, but it works!

I'm not kidding when I say that post-its were, and still are, some of the most important supplies I used during my recovery; but in the next chapter, we'll take a look at a broader list of supplies that are helpful to have on hand.

KEY TAKEAWAYS

─────────────────────

✓ Wisdom and guidance don't often just show up out of nowhere, especially when you are struggling.

✓ Get one step ahead of yourself by putting up little notes to yourself with reminders of the things you need to hear.

✓ Be unapologetic about this. Go wild.

Chapter 11

Supplies

"The best way out is always through." –Robert Frost

When it comes to supplies for recovery, there are a few items that made a major difference for me. Here are my personal must-haves:

Eye Mask

A high-quality eye mask is still everything to me. For a long while, I used one that I picked up at Walgreens that was uncomfortable. Also, it didn't fully block out the light. When I finally upgraded, I wished I hadn't waited so long. I use a mask from the brand Asutra that I got on Amazon. It gently forms to fit your face, fully blocks the light, and has a gentle lavender scent. (I am very sensitive to smells, and this is a very clean/pure smell that does not trigger headaches for me). It also comes with a cooling gel insert that is lovely to use. As an added bonus, Asutra is a woman-owned business based in my adopted hometown of Chicago. I love supporting them.

Ear Plugs

Ear plugs are a must-have. I use the cheap foam ones, but I know many people love Loop brand. I use them at home and also keep them in my purse for when I am out and about.

Weighted Blanket

A friend gifted me with a weighted blanket in the early days of my recovery to help with sleep, and it is a treasure. It helped calm me at night and did help with sleep, and I also used it during the days while I was resting on the couch. It helps decrease my anxiety and gives me an overall feeling of comfort. I still use it today.

Fitness Tracker

I use a Fitbit for this. The heart rate monitor allows me to keep an eye on my heart rate during my walks for targeted exercise therapy, and the sleep feature helps me keep an eye on my sleep quality and duration. I also enjoy the exercise tracking feature so that I can get "credit" for my walks. You may benefit from higher quality, doctor ordered heart rate or sleep monitoring, but for at home purposes, this is a good place to start. There are many options available for fitness trackers at all price points.

Magnesium Cream

I waited a long while before purchasing "Melt Away Pain Magnesium Body Butter" (also by Asutra) because of the price tag, but once I got it, I wanted to buy a container for every room in the house. It is soothing, has a lovely gentle scent, and really makes a difference in relieving my neck and shoulder pain. I am obsessed with this stuff.

Homeopathic Pain Relief Gel

I also love the Arnicare topical pain reliever gel for neck pain. I get it at Target. It is cooling and gentle and does not have the menthol scent like many other topical pain relievers.

BioFreeze

The sensation of this product is cooling and a bit more intense than the Magnesium Cream or Homeopathic Gel, both of which are quite soothing. I used it on days when my neck pain required something stronger.

Cold & Hot Packs

I use these on my face, head, neck, and shoulders. I have a set of different sized, bean-bag type packs that can double for both hot and cold use. There are also some cool "headache hats" available that cover and ice your whole head at the same time, and bandanas that can be used on both the head and neck. There are lots of options on Amazon.

High Quality Pillow

I use a pillow recommended by a musculoskeletal specialist. With neck injuries and whiplash being so common alongside concussion, having a pillow that supports your neck is very important. This is something you could source from a chiropractor or upper cervical specialist.

Noise Canceling Headphones

I was never willing to spend the money for a pair of my own, but I borrowed a pair from a friend for a while and absolutely loved them. They helped drown out household sounds when friends were over helping with meal prep, dishes, phone calls, etc. They also helped instill a sense of calm when I had them on. There are options available at many different price points, so if you shop around, you should be able to find a pair that fits your needs.

Grocery Delivery Service

For a long time, I was unable to handle going into stores. The lights, noise, motion, and visual overwhelm made me nauseous, dizzy, dazed, and flared my headaches significantly. Friends and family often helped by delivering groceries, but I also relied on online services like Instacart and Amazon. Sometimes I was in too much pain to utilize the online ordering system and would call a friend and have them do it for me. Most online services save your purchase histories, so it's easy to scroll through and simply click to reorder your usuals. Now that I am in a better place, I primarily use the order pickup option to save myself from the energy drain of going into the store.

I also crowd-sourced a list of favorite supplies from a number of Facebook groups. The most common responses I got were noise-canceling headphones, earplugs, and weighted blankets. Here are a few more frequent responses:

- Sunglasses

- Essential oils

- Acupressure mat

- Daily pill organizer

- Blue light glasses and blue light filters on phone and laptop

For quick links to my suggested products, visit www.theconcussioncompanion.com/supplies.

At this point, we have covered the big picture of recovery, the essentials for healing, and tools and resources for getting through the days. In the next chapter we will wrap it all up and get you back to the work of healing.

KEY TAKEAWAYS

✓ Take a few minutes to put together a list of items that will support your pain management, stress management, and nervous system. These things will help set you up for success.

✓ Experiment with some of the items I have suggested, or have a friend or family member help you research what will work best for you.

Chapter 12

Final Thoughts

"It's lack of faith that makes people afraid of meeting challenges, and I believed in myself." –Muhammad Ali

As we close things out, I want to remind you that you have everything inside you that you need to carry yourself through this—the fire, the desire, the wisdom, and the drive to guide yourself powerfully through your recovery. How do I know? Because you picked up this book. You *finished* this book. You are here, you are showing up for yourself, and that is no small thing.

I hope what you learned in these chapters will help light your path forward. I encourage you to keep this book handy as a guide and to come back to the sections you need again and again any time you need. I also want to encourage you to share this with your friends and family so they can support you better along the way, too.

Lastly, I want to share a note I wrote for myself during my darkest days. I wrote this to remind myself that, despite the pain, I still had most of my health, and I still had a future. I bumped up against all sorts of internal resistance every time I read it, but that was the point. I needed the reminder that these things were true even when it didn't feel like it. This one lived as a note on my phone, so I could review it at any time. I hope you will take the spirit of this note and create something similar for yourself if you need a reminder, too. Here is my note to self:

> *You have a brain injury, yes.*
> *But you are alive.*
> *You are recovering.*
> *You are strong, and*
> *you will be okay.*

> *You will come out stronger, braver, wiser than before.*
> *Keep your head up.*
> *Do the next right thing.*
> *Be kind to yourself.*
> *Practice compassion.*
> *Choose gratitude.*
> *Keep going.*
> *You've got this.*

Above all else, I want to remind you to keep moving forward, keep being good to yourself, and keep believing in your body and your recovery. Trust that the answers are on the way and that progress will unfold. You are doing so great. Keep going, my friend.

I am sending so many good vibes and well wishes to you. Thank you for letting me and my story be part of yours.

Thanks for Reading

THE
CONCUSSION
Companion

I hope the concepts I shared are helpful to you or someone you love. If you enjoyed this book, I would love to hear about it in a review. Reviews are always welcome.

Thank You!

If you would like to stay up to speed on my latest work or learn about my private coaching program, let's connect. You can get in touch with me at:
www.theconcussioncompanion.com

E-mail: hello@theconcussioncompanion.com
Instagram: @theconcussioncompanion

I have included a list of the additional resources, books, and online education programs I mentioned throughout the book in the next section. I hope you find them helpful. I wish you all the best in your recovery.

Stacey

Don't forget!

P.S.: Don't forget your free bonus, **The Companion Workbook.** You can still claim yours today by visiting www.theconcussioncompanion.com/freebonus.

Resources

Books

Concussion Rescue: A Comprehensive Program to Heal Traumatic Brain Injury by Dr. Kabran Chapek

How to Feed A Brain by Cavin Balaster

How to Sleep Smarter by Shawn Stevenson

Meditation for Fidgety Skeptics by Dan Harris and Jeff Warren

My Stroke of Insight by Dr. Jill Bolte-Taylor

The Against All Grain cookbook series by Danielle Walker

The Concussion Repair Manual: A Practical Guide to Recovering from Traumatic Brain Injury by Dr. Dan Engle

Online Education Programs

Concussion Compass
www.concussioncompass.com

The Concussion Community
www.theconcussioncommunity.com

The Concussion Fix

www.concussiondoc.io/courses/the-concussion-fix

The LoveYourBrain Foundation

www.loveyourbrain.com

Provider Locators

Brain Injury Association of America state-by-state resources

www.biausa.org/find-bia

CLF Concussion Clinic Finder

www.concussionfoundation.org/concussion-clinics-finder

Complete Concussion Management Clinic Finder

www.clinics.completeconcussions.com

CLF Concussion Helpline

www.concussionfoundation.org/helpline

BetterHelp

www.betterhelp.com

Psychology Today

www.psychologytoday.com

Acknowledgments

Love and thanks forever and ever to everyone who participated in my recovery journey and supported me along the way, with special thanks to:

Elaine Smith, Jane Smith, and Stephanie Mathews. The indomitable, indefatigable trio. My rocks and life advisors in chief.

My relatives and friends who never stopped checking in and offered their endless support. To the core team: Katie DeGroote, Shelli DiFranco, Katelynd Duncan, Olivia Johnson, Michael Marino, Matt Maxwell, Allison Osborne, Jayna Smith, Stephanie Spiewak, Evan Trad, and Book Club. Holy cow, you guys. That was an epic mess. Thank you for carrying me through it. I will never have enough words of love or gratitude for you. You are truly exceptional humans, and I am so grateful to be in your orbits.

To every single person who supported my GoFundMe, thank you so much. You made my recovery, my future, and this book possible.

Every medical provider that I have worked with. Special thanks to Eve Brownstone, Kate Davey, Dr. Laurel Griffin, Dr. Sashil Kapur, Jakub Koziol, Mike Morrow, and Dr. Dori

Moskowitz for your outstanding, effective, compassionate work. And to Dr. Kaz Nelson for stepping in when the wheels came off.

Ellen Butler and Nina Figueroa for your invaluable input and feedback. Brett Hilker, the Self-Publishing School team, and Jeannie Culbertson for helping bring this project to life and completion. You are each outstanding and a joy to work with.

The two paramedics who helped me to the hospital in February 2021. I don't know your names, but your patience, kindness, and gentleness will stay with me forever.

To every advocate who is doing work in the concussion space: I can't wait to join you.

Notes

1 Gail Hayes, "Press Release," Centers for Disease Control and Prevention (Centers for Disease Control and Prevention, June 7, 2007), https://www.cdc.gov/media/pressrel/2007/r070607.htm.

2 "What Is a Concussion?," What is a Concussion? | Concussion Legacy Foundation, accessed September 2, 2022, https://concussion-foundation.org/concussion-resources/what-is-concussion

3 Christa Hillstrom, "The Hidden Epidemic of Brain Injuries from Domestic Violence," The New York Times (The New York Times, March 1, 2022), https://www.nytimes.com/2022/03/01/magazine/brain-trauma-domesticviolence.html.

4 "Concussion Alliance," Concussion Alliance, accessed September 2, 2022, https://www.concussionalliance.org/.

5 "How Long Will It Take Me to Recover from a Concussion?," Brain Injury Association of America, August 4, 2020, https://www.biausa.org/brain-injury/about-brain-injury/nbiic/how-long-will-it-take-me-to-recover-from-aconcussion.

6 Kabran Chapek and Daniel G. Amen, *Concussion Rescue: A Comprehensive Program to Heal Traumatic Brain Injury* (New York, NY: Citadel Press, 2020).

7 Kabran Chapek and Daniel G. Amen, *Concussion Rescue: A Comprehensive Program to Heal Traumatic Brain Injury* (New York, NY: Citadel Press, 2020).

8 Beaumont, Neurology | What to Expect After a Concussion |
Beaumont Health, accessed September 2, 2022, https://www.beau-
mont.org/conditions/what-to-expect.

9 Neil Craton, Haitham Ali, and Stephane Lenoski, "Coach CV: The
Seven Clinical Phenotypes of Concussion," Brain sciences (MDPI,
September 16, 2017), https://www.ncbi.nlm.nih.gov/pmc/articles/
PMC5615260/.

10 Sandel, *Shaken Brain,* 2020.

11 "CDC: 6 Percent of Americans Engage in These 5 Health-Related
Behaviors," CBS News (CBS Interactive, May 27, 2016), https://
www.cbsnews.com/minnesota/news/cdc-6-percent-of-americans-en-
gage-in-these-5-health-relatedbehaviors/.

12 Kory Taylor and Elizabeth B. Jones, "Adult Dehydration - Statpearls
- NCBI Bookshelf," National Library of Medicine, May 15, 2022,
https://www.ncbi.nlm.nih.gov/books/NBK555956/.

13 "The Water in You: Water and the Human Body Completed," Water
Science School, May 22, 2019, https://www.usgs.gov/special-topics/
water-science-school/science/water-you-water-and-human-body.

14 "How Sleep Deprivation Can Cause Inflammation," Harvard
Health, January 11, 2022, https://www.health.harvard.edu/sleep/
how-sleep-deprivation-can-cause-inflammation.

15 David Perlmutter and Austin Perlmutter, *Brain Wash: Detox Your
Mind for Clearer Thinking, Deeper Relationships and Lasting Happiness*
(New York, NY: Little, Brown Spark, 2021).

16 "Antioxidants," The Nutrition Source, March 3, 2021, https://www.
hsph.harvard.edu/nutritionsource/antioxidants/.

17 Monica AlgaeCal, "2022 Dirty Dozen and Clean Fifteen Lists - and the Impact on Bone Health!," AlgaeCal, July 28, 2022, https://blog.algaecal.com/infographic-dirty-dozen-clean-fifteen/.

18 Engle, *The Concussion Repair Manual*, 2017.

19 Cavin Balaster, *How to Feed a Brain: Nutrition for Optimal Brain Function and Repair* (Austin, TX: Feed A Brain LLC, 2017).

20 Kira M. Newman, "How Journaling Can Help You in Hard Times," Greater Good, August 18, 2020, https://greatergood.berkeley.edu/article/item/how_journaling_can_help_you_in_hard_times.

21 BA Madhuleena Roy Chowdhury, "The Neuroscience of Gratitude and How It Affects Anxiety & Grief," PositivePsychology.com, April 9, 2019, https://positivepsychology.com/neuroscience-of-gratitude/.

22 Glennon Doyle, *Untamed* (Dial Press, 2020).

23 Dan Harris, Jeff Warren, and Carlye Adler, *Meditation for Fidgety Skeptics: A 10% Happier How-to Book* (London: Yellow Kite, 2020).

24 Jill Bolte Taylor, *My Stroke of Insight: A Brain Scientist's Personal Journey* (New York, NY: Penguin Books, 2016

Made in the USA
Monee, IL
12 November 2024

69970416R00125